LANCASHIRE COUNTY LIBRARY
D0521931
30118138589712

Lancashire Library Services	
30118138589712	
PETERS	J600LOU
£9.99	14-Nov-2019
CLE	

CHILDREN'S ENCYCLOPEDIA OF TECHNOLOGY

Anita Loughrey and Alex Woolf

ARCTURUS

Picture Credits:
Every attempt has been made to clear copyright. Should there be any inadvertent omission, please apply to the publisher for rectification.
Key: b-bottom, t-top, c-centre, l-left, r-right

Alamy: 19tl; **Dr. Dietrich Matthes:** 51bl; **Dreamstime:** 52-53 (Stepan Popov); **EUMETSAT:** 63tr; **Getty Images:** 89br; **Hallbauer & Fioretti:** 104bl; **iStockphoto:** 95br; **Jaap Haartson:** 28bl; **Liebherr-International Deutschland GmbH (Biberach an der Riß):** 108bl; **Martin Sanders - Beehive Illustration:** 10bl, 16c, 17t, 20b, 33cr, 44cl, 49bl, 64cr, 70tr, 74c, 76b, 77b, 85c, 88t, 92br, 104bl, 108cl, 110c, 112-113b, 114c; **Met Office © Crown copyright:** 62br; **NASA:** 24tr, 25tr, 25bl; **Science Photo Library:** 37br; **Shutterstock:** cover, 4-5, 4bl, 5tr, 6-7c, 6tr, 6cl, 7tr, 8c, 8bl, 9cr, 9tl, 10c, 11cr, 11bl, 12-13, 12cl, 12cr, 13tr, 14bl, 15c, 16-17, 17bl, 18-19 (FotograFFF), 18bl, 20-21, 20cl, 21tr, 22-23, 22cl, 24-25, 26-27, 26bc, 27tl, 27bl, 28-29, 28cl, 28tr, 29br, 29tr, 30-31, 30bl, 31cr, 32-33, 32cl, 32bl, 33br, 34-35, 34c, 34tr, 35br, 36-37, 36cl, 36cr, 38-39, 38bl, 38tr, 39tr (katacarix), 39cr, 40-41, 40c, 42-43, 42bl (Wachiwit), 43cr, 44-45, 44cr, 45tr, 46-47, 46cr, 46cl, 46tr, 48-49 (Dedi Grioroiu), 48c, 48bl, 50-51 (Denys Prykhodov), 50tr, 50bl, 51tl, 52cr, 52br, 52cl, 54-55, 54cl, 55bl, 56-57, 57cr, 58-59, 58cl, 58c, 59cl (fyv6561), 60-61, 60cl, 62-63, 62c, 64-65, 65tl, 66-67, 66ct, 66bl, 67t, 68-69, 68tr, 68b, 70-71, 70cl, 70b, 70tc, 72-73, 72c, 72br, 74-75, 75tl, 75bl, 76-77, 78-79, 78c, 79tr, 79br, 80-81, 80-81, 80bl81br, 81tl, 82-83, 82cl, 82tr, 84-85, 84br, 86-87, 86bl, 87tr, 87br, 88-89, 89tr, 90-91, 90bl, 90c, 92-93, 92tr, 92b, 93b, 93tl, 94-95, 94c, 94bl, 96-97, 96bl, 97tr, 98-99, 98bl, 99tr, 99bl, 99tl, 100-101, 100bl, 101tl, 101bl, 102-103, 102c, 102bl, 103cr, 104-105, 104cr, 105tl, 105b, 106-107, 106tr, 106cr, 106bl, 107tr, 108-109, 109tr, 110-111, 111cr (Pavel L Photo and Video), 112-113, 112-113b, 112tr, 113cr, 114-115, 114-115, 115tr, 116-117, 116bl, 117t, 118-119, 118bl, 119tl, 119cr, 120-121, 120cl, 120tr, 120bl, 121tr, 122-123, 122cl, 122tr, 122bl, 124-125 (Anton Gvozdikov), 124bl, 125cr (Pack-Shot); **Timoni West:** 44bl; **US Navy**: 64bl; **Wellcome collection:** 36bl, 69tl, 87tl, 91bl, 97bl; **Wikimedia commons:** 6bl (Birmingham Museums Trust), 12bl (CAEV.weebly.com), 15bl (Imperial War Museums), 16bl (Dibner Library of the History of Science and Technology), 21bl, 23bl (Smithsonian Institution), 31bl, 34bl (Smithsonian Institution), 39bl (US Library of Congress), 40bl (IEEE), 43tl, 47bl (ALJAWAD), 53tl (Jeri Ellsworth), 54bl (Gage Skidmore), 57br (Paul Clarke), 58bl (US National Library of Medicine), 61tr (SA Torchi), 63bl (ITU Pictures), 67bl, 71bl (Post of Romania), 72bl, 77tl, 78bl, 82bl (lloydcopeman.com), 84bl, 88bl (George Grantham Bain Collection, US Library of Congress), 110bl, 113tl, 114bl (Pangog 200), 117bl (Smithsonian, Institution), 119bl (US Library of Congress), 125bl (Www3cubed).

ARCTURUS
This edition published in 2019 by Arcturus Publishing Limited
26/27 Bickels Yard, 151–153 Bermondsey Street,
London SE1 3HA

Copyright © Arcturus Holdings Limited

All rights reserved. No part of this publication may be reproduced, stored in a retrieval system, or transmitted, in any form or by any means, electronic, mechanical, photocopying, recording or otherwise, without prior written permission in accordance with the provisions of the Copyright Act 1956 (as amended). Any person or persons who do any unauthorised act in relation to this publication may be liable to criminal prosecution and civil claims for damages.

Consultant: Anne Farthing
Authors: Anita Loughrey and Alex Woolf
Designer: Lorraine Inglis
Picture Editors: Paul Futcher and Lorraine Inglis
Editors: Becca Clunes and Joe Harris

ISBN: 978-1-78888-645-1
CH006561UK
Supplier 29, Date 0519, Print run 8461

Printed in China

In this book, one billion means one thousand million (1,000,000,000) and one trillion means one million million (1,000,000,000,000).

CHILDREN'S

ENCYCLOPEDIA OF TECHNOLOGY

CONTENTS

Introduction

Technology is the use of scientific knowledge to create products to make our lives easier and solve problems. Throughout history people have invented tools, machines, and electrical devices that help us in our everyday life.

Identifying a need

Technology is developed to meet our needs. For example, we all need water to survive. Instead of going down to the river every time we need a drink, technology makes our lives easier by bringing water straight into our kitchens with pipes and indoor plumbing.

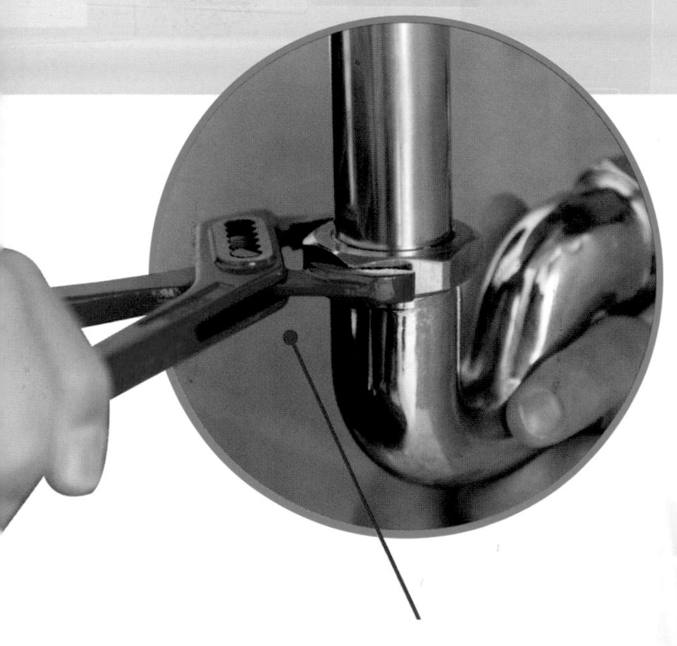

Tools, like this spanner, are a form of technology.

Someone who designs a product is called an inventor.

Progress

Technology is always changing and advancing as our needs and demands increase. There is always another problem to solve.

Before automated electric street lights, we had gas-powered street lamps. Each lamp had to be lit by hand every night.

Design process

Once somebody has come up with an idea, they draw a design to show how their idea is going to work. To do this, inventors use their knowledge of physics and chemistry. They think about forces when deciding how the product will work and the properties of different materials to decide what materials would be best to use.

Bicycles

Bicycles use pedals to drive a chain, which moves the wheels and propels the bicycle forward. Gears change the distance the bike moves forward with each pedal stroke. They enable the rider to maintain a comfortable pedalling speed, whether cycling uphill, downhill, or on a level surface.

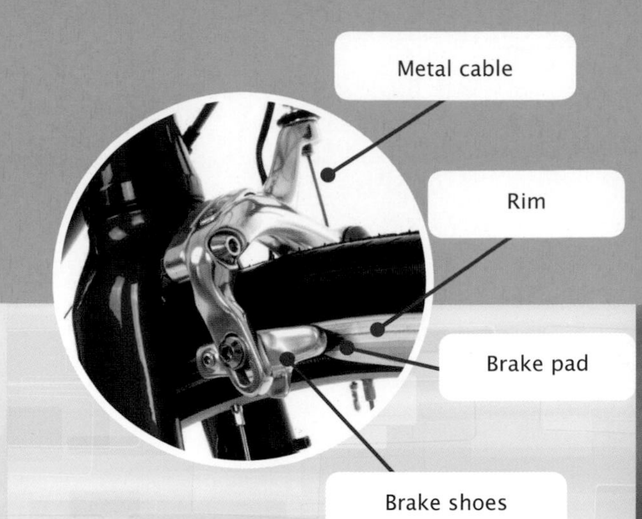
Metal cable
Rim
Brake pad
Brake shoes

Brakes

When you press the brake levers on the handlebars, thin metal cables running to the front and back wheels pull on the brake shoes. The brake shoes force the brake pads to press against the rims of the wheels. This friction slows the bicycle down.

Gears

Gears are a set of toothed wheels attached to the axle of the bike's rear wheel. The teeth slot into the chain, which turns the gear. The smallest gear is closest to the frame and needs the least pedalling force to turn it. This is often used when riding uphill. The largest gear needs the most pedalling force to turn it, so the bicycle will travel further with one rotation—useful when riding downhill.

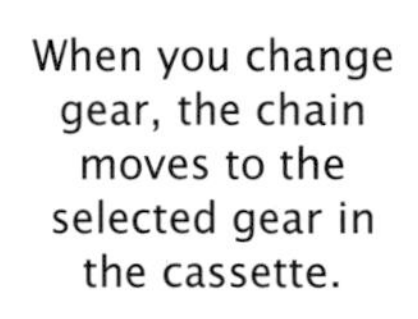

When you change gear, the chain moves to the selected gear in the cassette.

INVENTION

Inventor: John Kemp Starley

Invention: Rover Safety Bicycle

Date: 1885

The story: British inventor John Kemp Starley developed the modern design for a bicycle. It had equal-sized wheels, a chain to turn the rear wheel, and a steerable front wheel. It made the bicycle more stable than previous designs.

DID YOU KNOW? Olympic bicycles have wheels without spokes to improve airflow, reduce drag, and go faster. They do not have brakes.

The gear shifters are the controls that change the gears. They are attached to the derailleurs by gear cables.
Brake levers
Handlebars
Most bicycles have a "diamond" frame created with two triangles of hollow tube. The strong triangle shape supports the rider's weight between the back and front wheels.
Frame
Saddle
Gears
The back "derailleur" changes the gear by moving the bottom of the chain from side to side. It contains a spring to keep a constant tension on the chain.
Pedals
The front derailleur shifts the chain between the front wheel gears.
Chain
Wheels

Cars

A battery provides electricity for the spark to ignite the air and fuel mixture.

Cars are powered by an internal combustion engine, which produces energy by burning a mixture of compressed fuel and air. Sparks ignite the air fuel mix, pushing a set of pistons. The pistons rotate the crankshaft, which turns the driveshaft. The driveshaft is connected to the car's axle, causing the wheels to turn and moving the car forward.

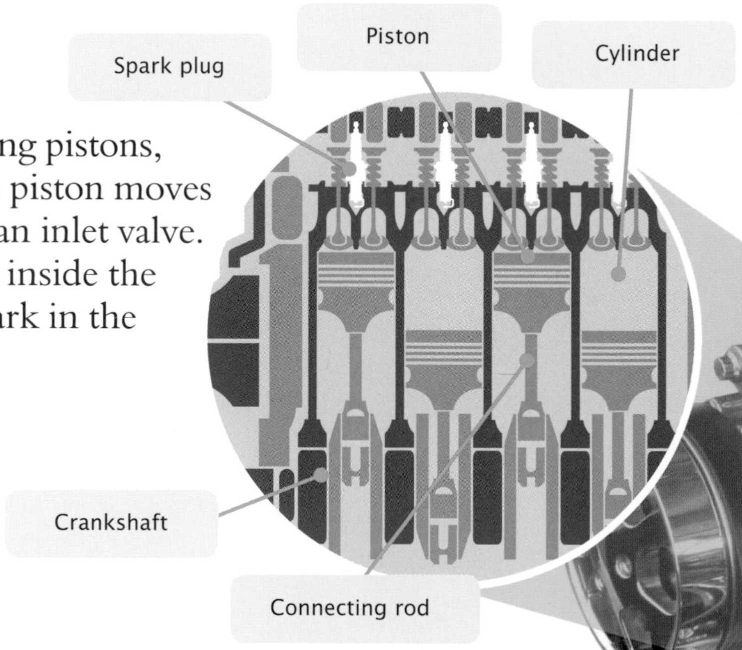

Four-stroke sequence

Inside the engine is a row of metal cylinders containing pistons, which move in a four-stroke sequence. 1 When the piston moves down, it drags fuel and air into the cylinder through an inlet valve. 2 When the inlet valve closes, the piston moves up inside the cylinder, compressing the fuel and air mixture. A spark in the spark plug ignites the mixture, producing hot gases.

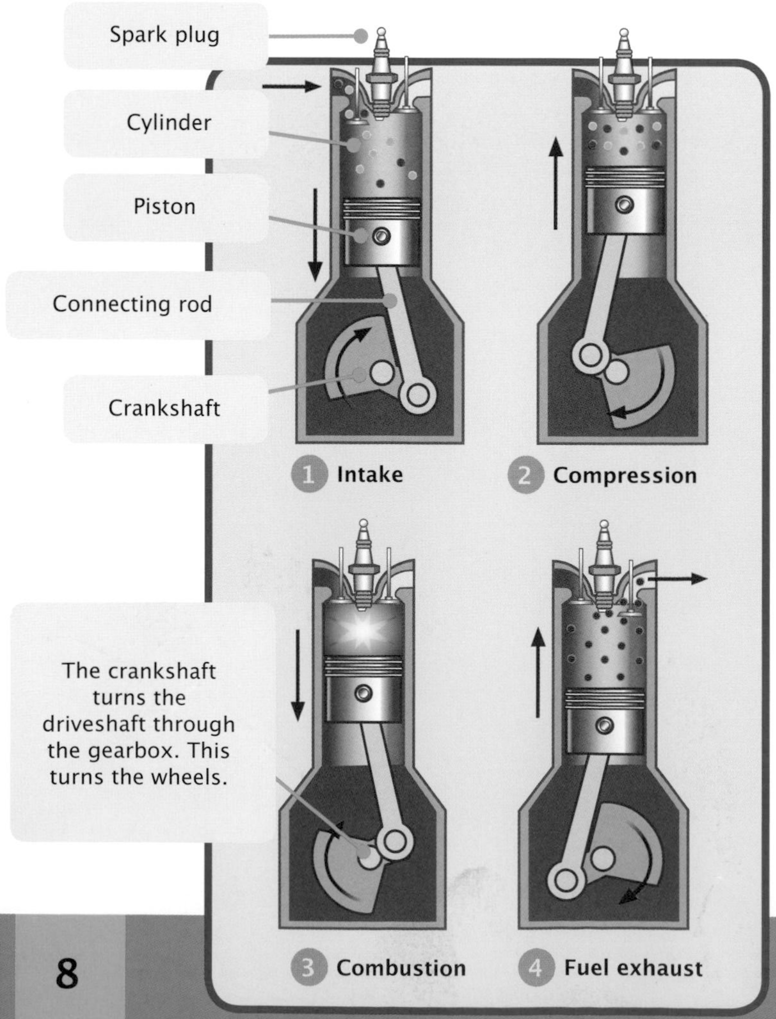

The crankshaft turns the driveshaft through the gearbox. This turns the wheels.

3 The hot gases expand, pushing the piston back down. When the piston hits the bottom, the exhaust valve opens, emptying the cylinder of waste gases.
4 Now the piston moves up again, ready for another cycle. The up-and-down movement of the pistons is turned into rotational movement by the crankshaft.

DID YOU KNOW? Today about 80 percent of a car is recyclable.

INVENTION

Inventor: Margaret A. Wilcox

Invention: Car heater

Date: 1893

The story: American mechanical engineer Margaret A. Wilcox developed a way to direct air from the engine inside the car to give heat. Her invention is the basis of car heaters today.

The engine sucks in air and fuel.
Oil allows the metal parts to move easily.
Water pumped from the radiator keeps the engine cool.

Car Safety

Some car safety features are designed to avoid collisions. These include mirrors, lights, horns, and anti-lock braking systems (ABS), which prevent wheels from locking and the car skidding during heavy braking. Other safety features are designed to protect the driver and passengers in the event of a collision. These include seatbelts and airbags.

An airbag is a life-saving cushion that inflates in 0.03 seconds. The airbag completely deflates by the time the car stops.

Airbags

An airbag has three parts: the bag itself, a sensor, and an inflation system. The nylon bag is fitted into the steering wheel, dashboard, or door. The sensor contains an accelerometer—a device for measuring the acceleration of a moving body. If the sensor detects a collision, it sends an electric current through a heating element in the inflation system. The heat causes two chemicals, sodium azide and potassium nitrate, to react, producing a blast of nitrogen gas that inflates the airbag.

The wheel speed sensor determines if the wheel is trying to lock up during braking.

If the wheel tries to lock up, hydraulic valves limit or reduce braking to prevent skidding.

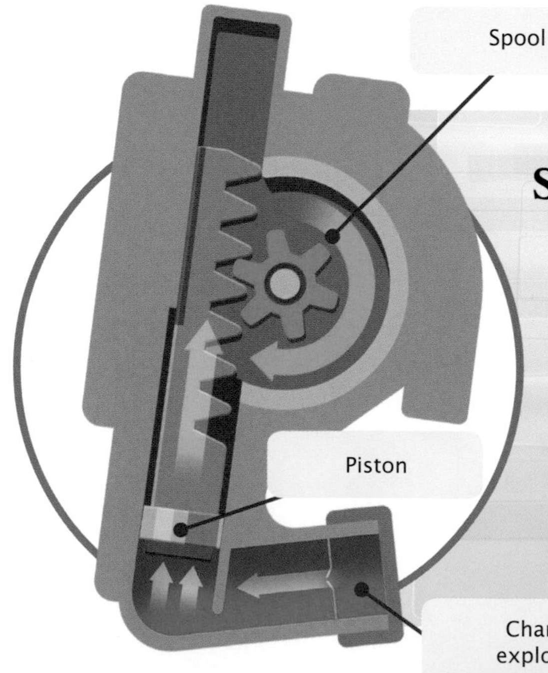

Spool
Piston
Chamber of explosive gas

Seatbelts

Inside the seatbelt casing is a "retractor mechanism" consisting of a spool and a spring. When the belt is pulled, the spool rotates and the spring untwists. When let go, the spring twists back, rotating the spool, and the belt tightens. The seatbelt also has a mechanism called a pre-tensioner with a chamber of explosive gas. In a crash, an electric current ignites the gas, pushing a piston that rotates the spool, tightening the belt.

DID YOU KNOW? The first cars had no steering wheel. People steered with a lever.

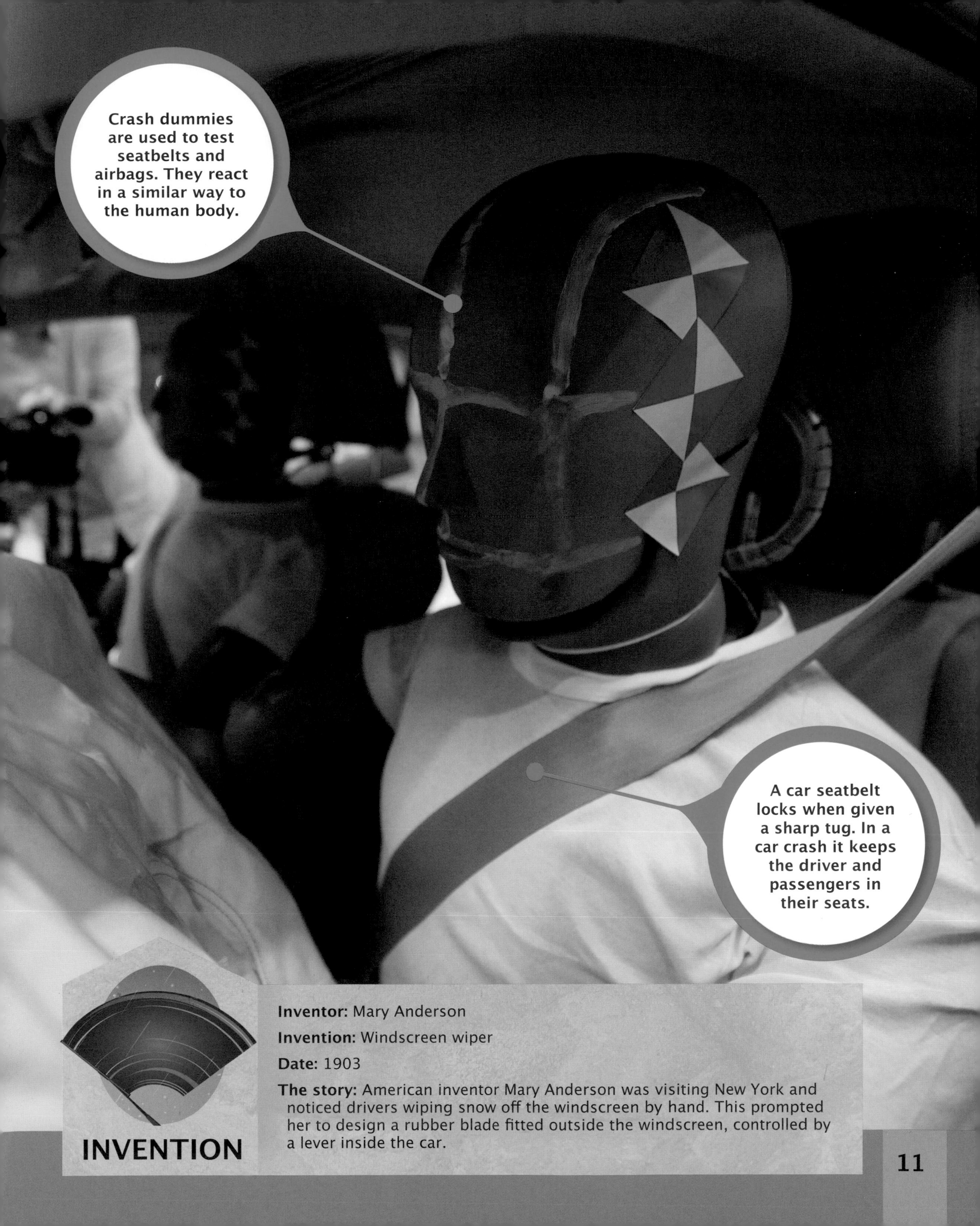
Crash dummies are used to test seatbelts and airbags. They react in a similar way to the human body.
A car seatbelt locks when given a sharp tug. In a car crash it keeps the driver and passengers in their seats.

INVENTION

Inventor: Mary Anderson

Invention: Windscreen wiper

Date: 1903

The story: American inventor Mary Anderson was visiting New York and noticed drivers wiping snow off the windscreen by hand. This prompted her to design a rubber blade fitted outside the windscreen, controlled by a lever inside the car.

Trains

Diesel trains contain a powerful two-stroke diesel engine. Unlike four-stroke car engines (see page 8), the pistons in diesel engines complete a two-stroke cycle and the fuel is injected directly into the compressed air. Electric trains often get their electricity from a third rail running alongside the track, which drives motors on their wheels.

Some trains have their electricity supplied by overhead cables.

Points

Points are the switches that enable the train to change tracks. Part of the track, called the blade, moves and guides the wheels at the junction where the tracks meet.

Blade

Under the tracks are sleepers. They keep the tracks the correct distance apart. The tracks are bolted to the sleepers.

Flange

Rail

INVENTOR

Inventor: Robert Davidson

Invention: Electric train

Date: 1837

The story: Scottish chemist Robert Davidson designed and made the first electric train. It had four wheels and was powered by batteries. The train was tested on the Edinburgh–Glasgow line in September 1842.

Signals

Signals tell the train driver when to stop and when it is safe to move. They are controlled automatically by computers in a control room. Before this they were operated by hand using levers. A lever would change the signal and move the points. Today, signals use red and green lights like traffic lights.

Trains have metal wheels with a rim on the inside called a flange. Flanges stop the wheels from slipping off the tracks.

DID YOU KNOW? The world's longest train journey is between Moscow and Pyongyang. It takes almost 8 days.

Planes

A plane creates lift with its wings, and thrust (forward motion) with its engines. A jet engine works on the same principle as a car engine: it burns fuel with air to release energy. But instead of using cylinders and pistons, a jet engine consists of one long metal tube. Air is drawn in at the front end, compressed by a fan, mixed with fuel, and combusted. Finally, it is blasted out the back as hot exhaust, creating thrust.

Turbo jet engine

A fan at the front of the jet engine sucks in cold air. Then a second fan called a compressor squeezes the air, increasing its temperature and pressure. Kerosene fuel is squirted into the engine, mixes with the compressed air, and combusts.

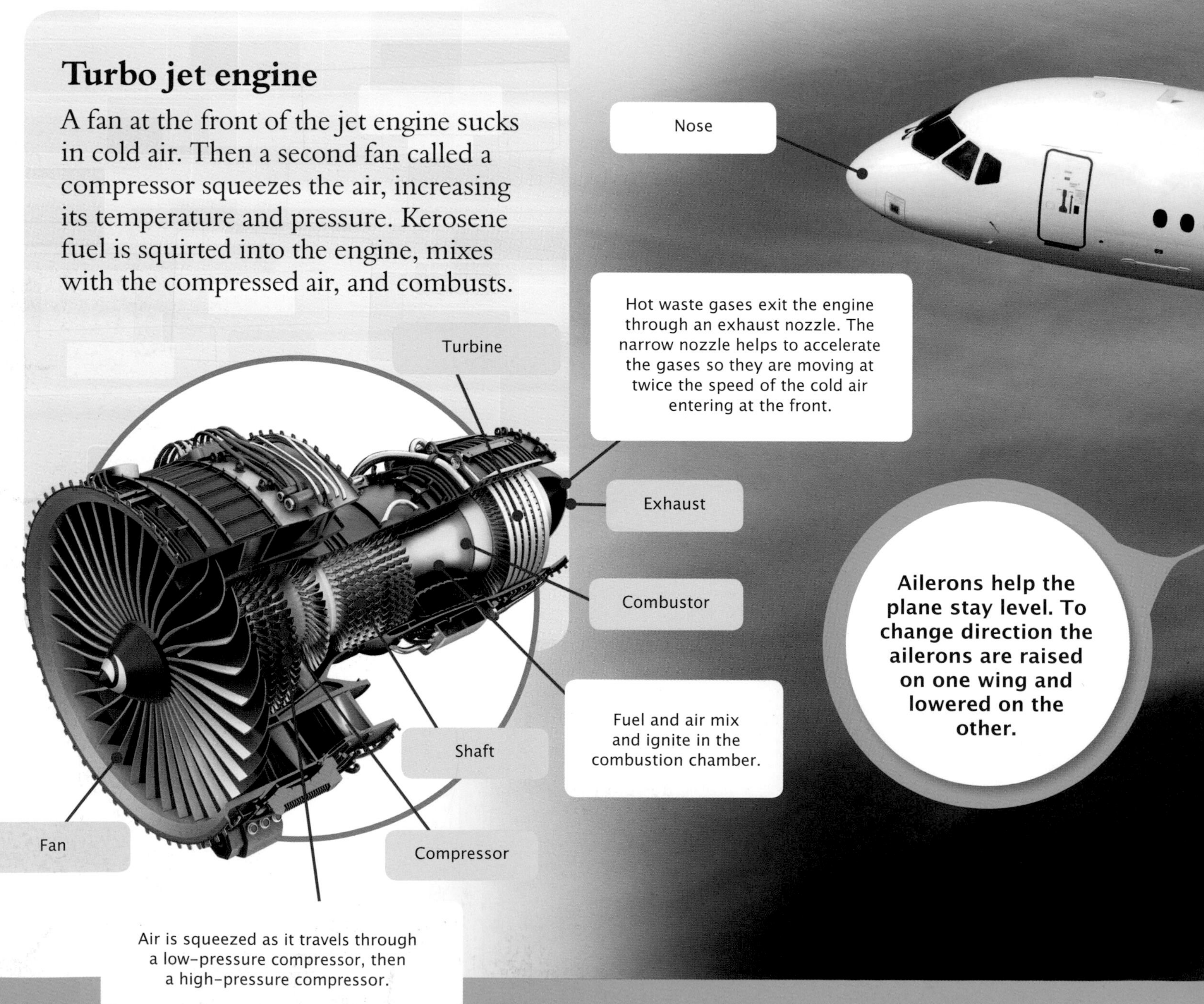

Nose
Turbine
Hot waste gases exit the engine through an exhaust nozzle. The narrow nozzle helps to accelerate the gases so they are moving at twice the speed of the cold air entering at the front.
Exhaust
Combustor
Ailerons help the plane stay level. To change direction the ailerons are raised on one wing and lowered on the other.
Fuel and air mix and ignite in the combustion chamber.
Shaft
Fan
Compressor
Air is squeezed as it travels through a low-pressure compressor, then a high-pressure compressor.

DID YOU KNOW? A flying boat called the *Spruce Goose* had a wingspan of 98 m (320 ft), the largest ever.

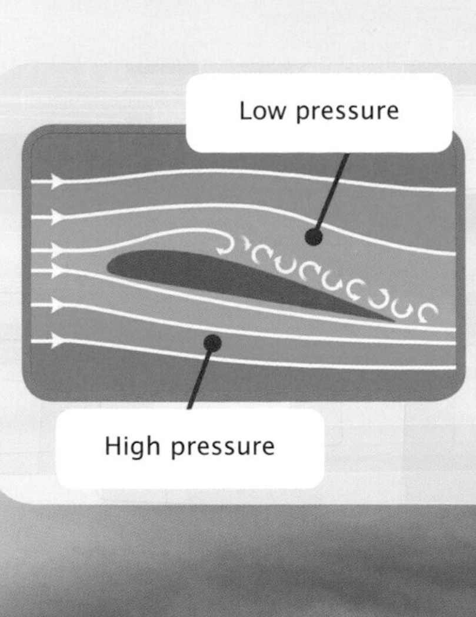
Low pressure
High pressure

Wings

The curved shape of the wing makes the pressure of the air travelling over it lower than the pressure of the air under the wing. The difference in pressure creates an upward force called lift.

The tail fin balances the position of the nose, keeping the plane level.
Wings
Slats provide more lift at lower speeds.
Rudder
Fuselage
Flaps increase lift during take-off and landing.
Tail fin
Spoilers act as brakes to create drag in order to slow the plane down.
The rudder works with the ailerons to turn the plane left or right
Jet engine

INVENTOR

Inventor: Sir Frank Whittle

Invention: Turbo jet engine

Date: 1930

The story: British pilot Frank Whittle designed the first turbo jet engine when he was in the RAF. After his first ideas were rejected, he worked on the problems until he had a workable model.

Speed Boats

As their name implies, speed boats are designed to go fast. Their hulls are made of light materials such as fibreglass, aluminium, or plywood, and have a streamlined shape. Their motors drive a propeller that pushes a jet of water out the back, giving the boat its thrust.

Outboard motor

An outboard motor is attached to the back of the hull with a clamp. It works in a similar way to a car engine. By opening up the throttle, the outboard motor burns more fuel and the propeller turns faster, increasing the speed.

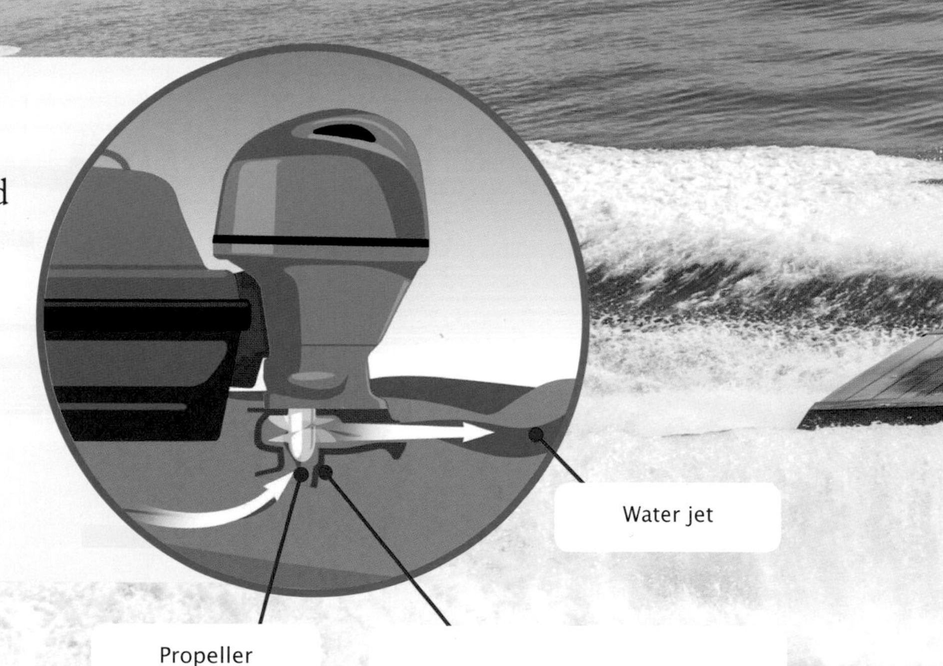
Water jet
Propeller
The propeller has angled blades to reduce turbulence in the water.

INVENTOR

Inventor: Josef Ressel

Invention: Screw propeller

Date: 1826

The story: Czech-Austrian inventor Josef Ressel came up with the idea to place a screw propeller onto a ship's steam engine. Early steamships used paddle wheels. Ressel's propeller gave ships more power and speed.

Inboard motor

An inboard motor is enclosed within the hull. The motor is connected to a driveshaft that spins the propeller. The engine is cooled by water pumped in from outside the boat. The water is then ejected out the back with the exhaust.

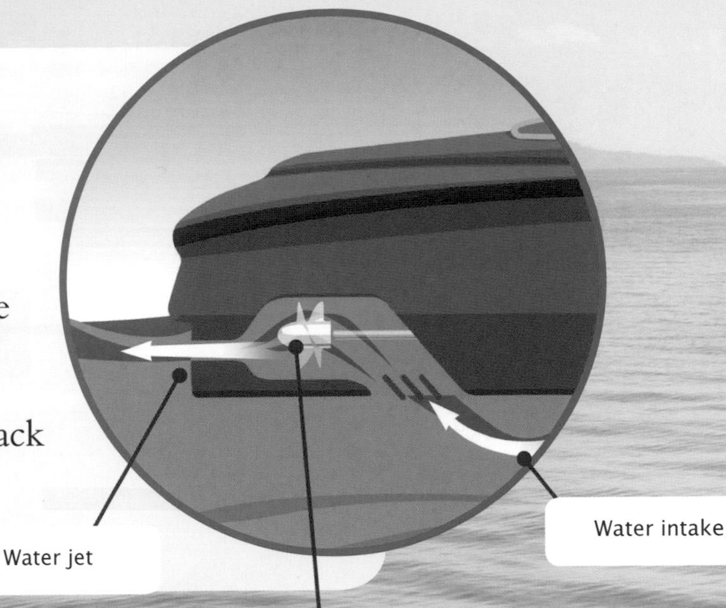
Water jet
Propeller
Water intake

The hull of a speed boat is designed to skim the surface of the water at high speeds.

Rudder

The rudder is the main method of steering a boat. It can be connected to the back of the boat or to the outboard motor. When the rudder is turned, it deflects the water and makes the boat change direction.

DID YOU KNOW? The first life jackets were made of cork.

Hovercraft

The hovercraft can travel over surfaces where other vehicles cannot go, including muddy ground, stormy water, and ice. It can even glide smoothly from the sea straight up onto a beach. It can do this because it levitates, or hovers, on a cushion of air.

Air flow

A hovercraft is quite a simple machine. A diesel or petrol engine powers a large downward-pointing fan. This fan creates the lift that raises the hovercraft above the surface. A rubber skirt traps a cushion of air under the craft.

Skirts can be simple, flexible rubber bags, or more complex designs with hundreds of "fingers" to maintain an even airflow.

Changing direction

The engine also powers other fans that propel the craft forward, backward, or sideways. A rudder positioned behind each fan changes the direction of the flow of air, enabling the hovercraft to turn.

INVENTOR

Inventor: Sir Christopher Cockerell

Invention: Hovercraft

Date: 1956

The story: British engineer Sir Christopher Cockerell was building cabin cruisers for holiday companies when he had the idea for the hovercraft. He used a can of cat food inside a coffee tin and reversed the air flow from a vacuum cleaner to prove his theory was correct. He tested it on the mud floor of his boatyard.

Ice has less friction, which means the hovercraft travels faster.

DID YOU KNOW? The average speed of a hovercraft is 56 km/h (35 mph).

Submarines

Submarines are designed to travel below water as well as on the surface. When on the surface, a submarine uses a diesel engine to work the propeller. When submerged, it is powered by a nuclear reactor or an electric motor.

Sonar

Light does not penetrate far underwater, so submarines navigate by sonar (standing for "sound navigation and ranging"). A sonar system emits pulses of sound waves through the water. These reflect off objects and their echoes return to the submarine, where they are picked up by sensitive microphones. A computer then uses these signals to construct a detailed image of a passing boat, sea creature, or the bottom of the ocean.

Ballast tank

Submarines can stay submerged for months at a time. They sink and float by emptying and refilling their ballast tanks with air or water.

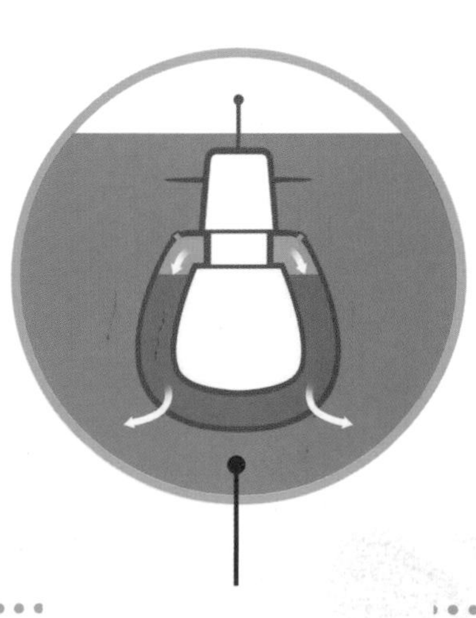

Water is taken in and the submarine sinks

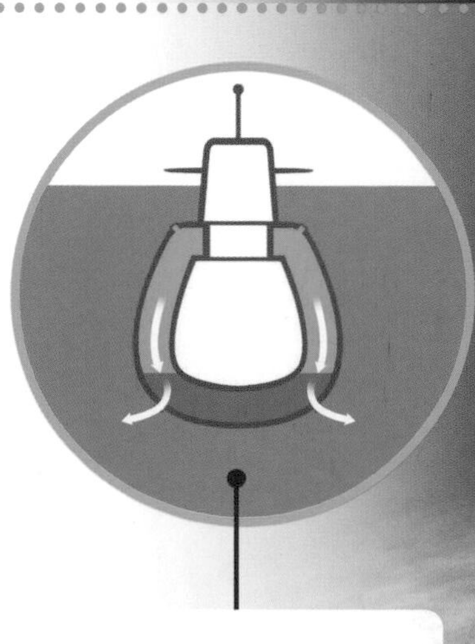

Air is pumped in, forcing the water out, and the submarine rises.

When the ballast tanks are filled with air, the submarine's weight drops until it is equal to the weight of the water it displaces. This causes the submarine to float to the surface.

A periscope is sometimes mounted on top of a raised tower called the conning tower. It lets the crew see above water when the submarine is submerged.

INVENTOR

Inventor: Cornelis Drebbel

Invention: Submarine

Date: 1620

The story: Dutch engineer Cornelis Drebbel built the first submarine that could be steered. The wooden frame covered with leather was powered by oars and the force of the current. It could remain submerged for about three hours.

DID YOU KNOW? Submarines do not have windows. They use underwater cameras instead.

Drones

Drones are unmanned aerial vehicles (UAVs). They can take off and land vertically, hover, and fly in different directions. Drone quadcopters are popular as they are easy to control and affordable.

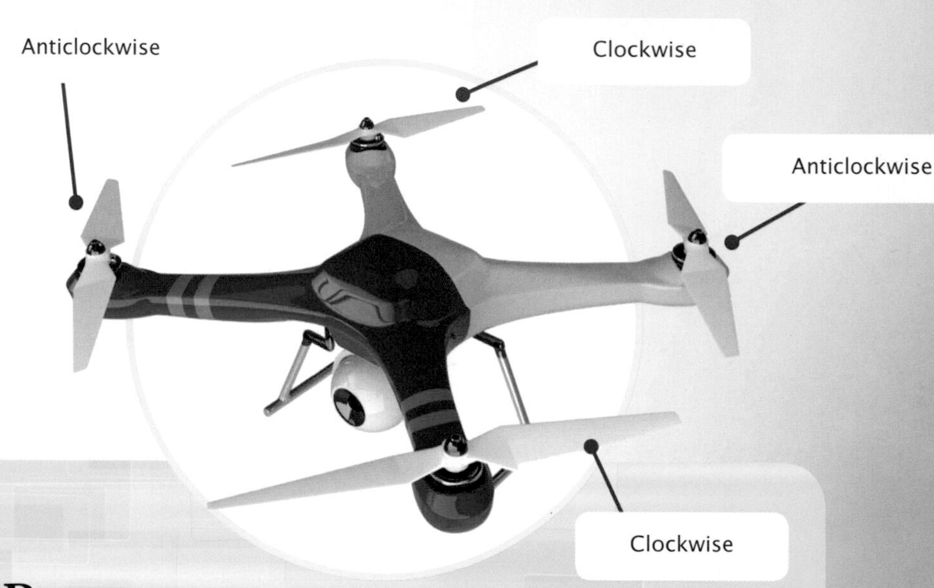

Anticlockwise
Clockwise
Anticlockwise
Clockwise

Quadcopter drones are controlled by remote control units that use radio waves. They can take the form of a gamepad, smartphone, tablet, or computer.

Rotors

The lift and thrust of a drone quadcopter is provided by four rotors that spin in different directions. They are mounted on spokes. As the rotor pushes down on the air, the air pushes up on the rotor. The faster the rotor spins, the greater the lift. To turn, one pair of rotors must spin slower than the other pair.

Sensors

On-board sensors keep the drones in the air. An altimeter tells the drone its height from the ground. GPS chips provide information on its position and direction of travel, and lets users set a return destination if the drone loses radio contact. Drones can also have laser or heat sensors.

DID YOU KNOW? The larger drones can withstand winds of 80 km/h (50 mph).

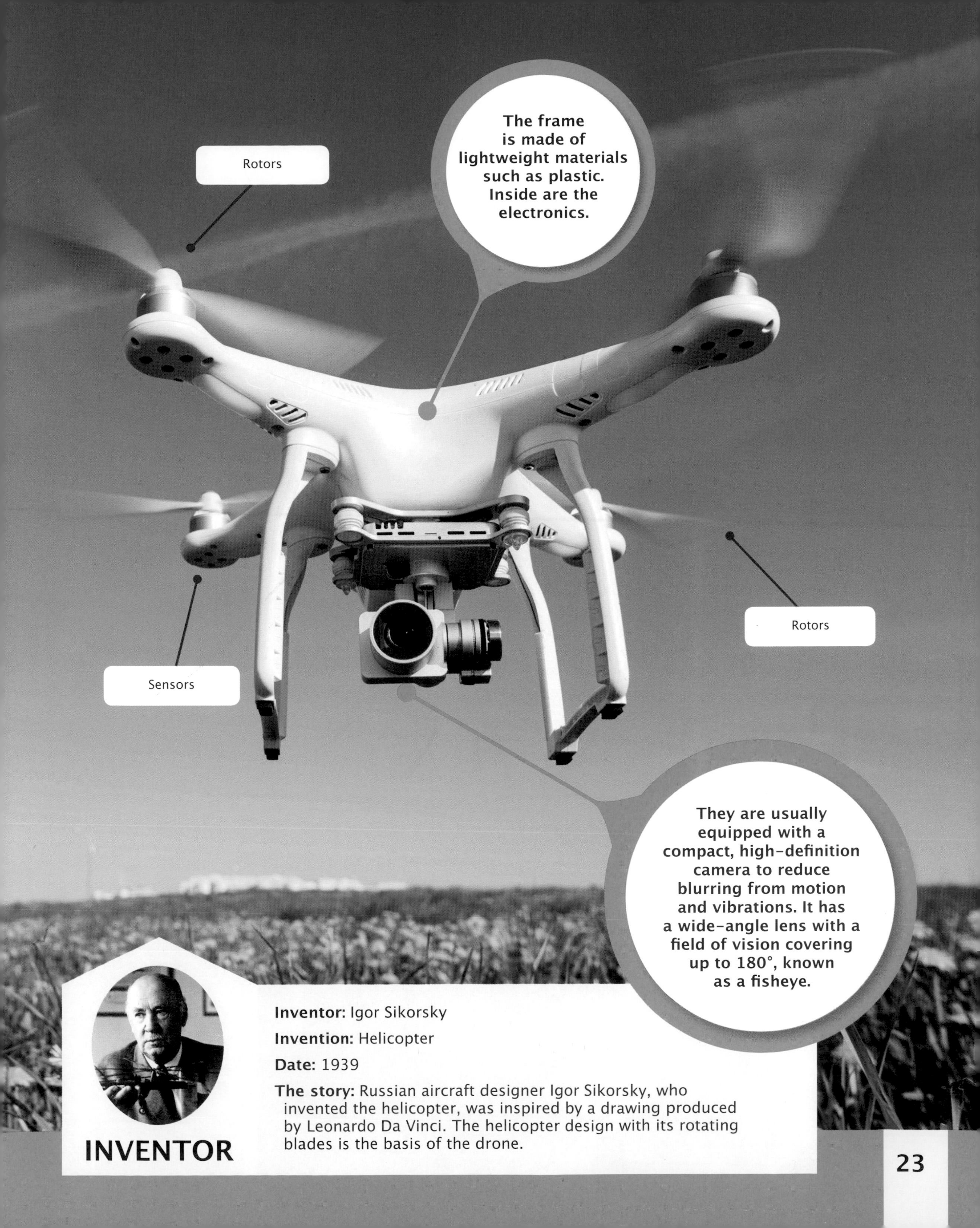
The frame is made of lightweight materials such as plastic. Inside are the electronics.
Rotors
Rotors
Sensors
They are usually equipped with a compact, high-definition camera to reduce blurring from motion and vibrations. It has a wide-angle lens with a field of vision covering up to 180°, known as a fisheye.

INVENTOR

Inventor: Igor Sikorsky

Invention: Helicopter

Date: 1939

The story: Russian aircraft designer Igor Sikorsky, who invented the helicopter, was inspired by a drawing produced by Leonardo Da Vinci. The helicopter design with its rotating blades is the basis of the drone.

Spacecraft

Today, thousands of spacecraft are circling the Earth, sending us data and relaying telecommunication signals. Robotic probes are being sent on missions to explore the planets, moons, comets, and asteroids of the solar system. The biggest spacecraft ever built is the International Space Station (ISS), currently in orbit around the Earth.

ISS structure

The ISS is made up of pressurized modules containing living quarters and laboratories for the astronauts, and solar arrays for power. It has six robotic arms used to carry out remote-controlled repairs and provide berths for arriving spacecraft.

Docking ports enable other spacecraft to connect to the space station.

DID YOU KNOW? The first space shuttle, called Columbia, was launched in 1981. It saw 22 years of service and completed 27 missions.

The Russian Soyuz spacecraft has taken people and supplies to and from the International Space Station.

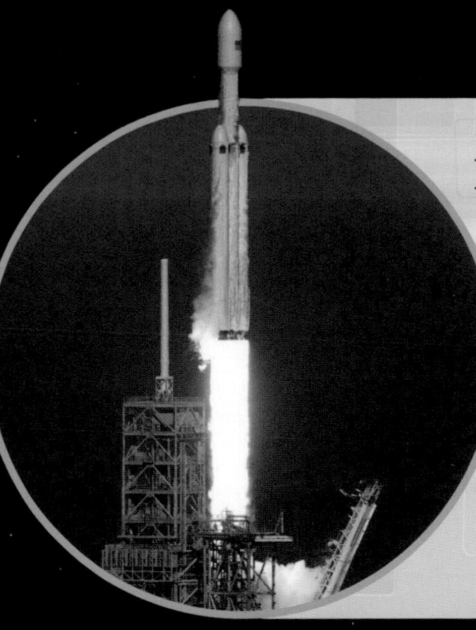

Falcon Heavy

In February 2018, SpaceX successfully launched the Falcon Heavy. The rockets descended to Earth in a controlled drop and landed vertically on the launch pad, ready to be reused. The Falcon Heavy is suitable for interplanetary missions.

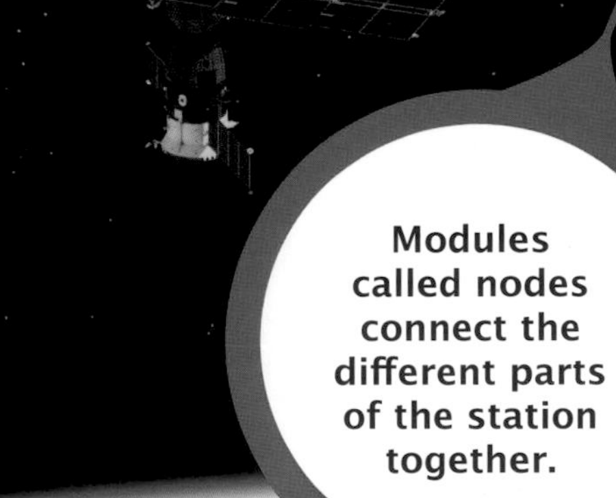

Modules called nodes connect the different parts of the station together.

INVENTOR

Inventor: Dr. Robert H. Goddard

Invention: First rocket to use liquid fuel

Date: March 26, 1926

The story: American physicist Dr. Robert H. Goddard invented the first rocket to use liquid fuel. Before this all rockets had been propelled by burning solid fuel. Goddard's rocket flew 56m at 100km/h (184ft at 62mph).

Three-dimensional (3D) Movies

Humans have stereoscopic vision. This means each eye sees a slightly different image. Each image is sent to the brain for processing and the brain combines the two images into one. This gives us greater depth perception than animals that have eyes on either side of their head. 3D technology uses the fact we have stereoscopic vision to create 3D images by sending slightly different pictures to each eye.

Polarized movies

Modern 3D movies use polarized light. Normal light is made up of waves that vibrate in multiple directions. Polarized light waves are filtered so they vibrate in only one direction. 3D movies are projected through different polarized filters, one sent to each eye.

Images sent to the right eye are polarized on the vertical plane.
Images sent to the left eye are polarized on the horizontal plane.
Each lens is filtered to let only one kind of polarized light through, so each eye sees a different version of the same frame. The brain combines them to create the illusion of 3D.

Active 3D television

With active 3D TV, images for left and right eyes are displayed alternately. This requires battery-powered "shutter" glasses with lenses coated with liquid crystal. Each lens quickly alternates between opaque and transparent, so each eye sees only the frame it's supposed to.

3D films are made using two camera lenses set side by side. Traditionally these had red and blue filters.

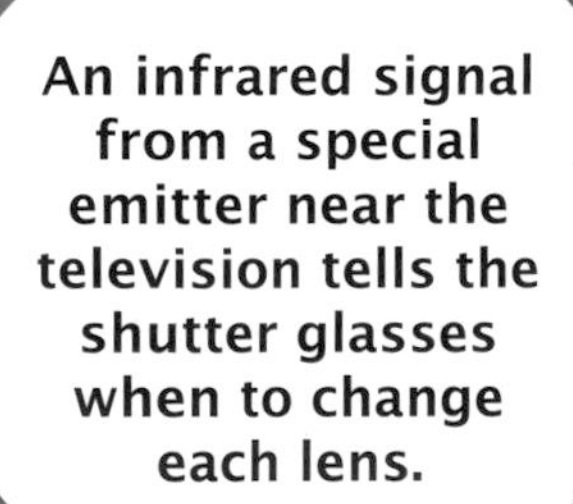

An infrared signal from a special emitter near the television tells the shutter glasses when to change each lens.

INVENTION

Inventor: Kenneth J. Dunkley

Invention: 3-DVG glasses

Date: 1986

The story: While researching human vision, American physicist Kenneth J. Dunkley found that by blocking two points in someone's peripheral (side) vision, he could transform 2D images into 3D images. His three-dimensional viewing glasses—3-DVG glasses—change ordinary photos into 3D.

DID YOU KNOW? Manufacturers are looking at building lenses into the screen to let viewers see 3D movies without glasses.

Bluetooth® Speakers

Bluetooth® speakers are wireless. They work by receiving radio signals from a smartphone or tablet. An antenna on the speakers detects the signals, and a receiver then converts them into electric signals, which a voice coil turns into sound vibrations. To work, the devices must first be paired. Once connected, the speakers will remember and recognize the device when it is within range.

Bluetooth® can be used for one-to-one device communication, or for sharing data between multiple devices.

Radio waves

Bluetooth® equipment transmits data via short-range radio waves that can connect to a wide variety of electronic devices. Because Bluetooth® uses radio waves, devices do not have to be in line of sight of each other.

You can instantly recognize if an electrical device has Bluetooth® capabilities because it will display the Bluetooth® symbol.

INVENTOR

Inventor: Jaap Haartsen

Invention: Bluetooth®

Date: 1994

The story: Dutch electrical engineer Jaap Haartsen was working in Sweden when he was asked to design a way smartphones could share data wirelessly. He described his idea as "a walkie-talkie done on a world-scale."

Files can be shared between devices using Bluetooth®.

Bluetooth® headset

A headset acts as both the transmitter and receiver of wireless signals. This lets people use their smartphones hands-free.

A Bluetooth® headset has a built-in speaker and microphone.

DID YOU KNOW? Bluetooth® was named after the Danish King Harald Bluetooth, who united Scandinavia during the tenth century.

Electric Guitars

When an electric guitar is plucked, the vibration is detected by a "pickup," which is a magnet wound with a coil of very fine wire. The pickup converts the vibration into an electric signal, which passes through a circuit that adjusts the signal's tone and volume. The signal then flows through an amplifier to a speaker that turns it into a sound.

Body

Bridge

Pickups

Pickups are electromagnets, mounted under the guitar's strings. Electromagnets turn motion into electric energy. Vibrations in the strings produce a corresponding vibration in the electromagnet's magnetic field, creating an electric signal.

Headstock and neck

The headstock contains the machine heads, which are used for tuning. The neck contains the fingerboard and frets to help the player know where to place their fingers to change a note.

The strings are tuned by tightening or loosening the machine heads.

The volume and tone controls adjust the frequency of the electric signal to produce different sounds.

Machine heads
Strings
Neck
Frets
Pickup
The amplifier boosts the electrical signal, so the electric guitar can be heard.
RHYTHM

INVENTOR

Inventor: Les Paul

Invention: A solid body electric guitar

Date: 1941

The story: American jazz guitarist Les Paul taught himself how to play the guitar. He was always inventing things and designed his own solid-body electric guitar.

DID YOU KNOW? The first electric guitar, called the Viv-tone, was invented in 1933 and was a big flop.

Headphones

Headphones work exactly like speakers, but they deliver sounds straight to the user's ears. Audio electric signals from the stereo are sent to electromagnets, called coils, inside the headphones. These turn the signals into motion, causing thin, flexible cones called diaphragms to vibrate. The vibrations create the sound waves that the user hears. Different sounds can be delivered to each ear to produce a stereo effect.

Earbuds

Earbuds work like headphones, but all the elements are much smaller. The coil is at the back of the earbud, and the diaphragm is near the front, often behind a layer of foam to protect your ears. The domed shape of the earbud shell helps to amplify the sound.

INVENTOR

Inventor: Nathaniel Baldwin

Invention: Headphones

Date: 1910

The story: American Nathaniel Baldwin sent the prototype for his headphone design to the US Navy. They were impressed with the quality of sound and requested more. However, he could accept orders of only 10 at a time because he was making them in his kitchen.

DID YOU KNOW? You should not play your music too loud through headphones because it can damage them and, more importantly, it can harm your hearing.

Active noise-cancellation (ANC) headphones

ANC headphones have microphones that measure ambient (background) noise. The headphones then create a sound with a waveform that is the exact negative of the ambient noise, cancelling it out.

1 Microphones detect ambient sound.
2 Sound is sent to the ANC circuitry.
3 The ANC circuitry creates inverted sound wave, cancelling ambient noise.
4 The ANC circuitry sends clear sound to speakers.
Padded cover
Diaphragm
Magnet
Coil

Closed-back headphones are sealed at the back, blocking out ambient noise and leaking less sound, but many people prefer the sound produced by open-back headphones.

Radios

Radio stations use antennae to send signals through the air carried by radio waves called carrier waves. This process is called modulation. There are two types of modulation: frequency modulation (FM), when the carrier wave's frequency (the number of waves per second) is altered; amplitude modulation (AM), when the wave's size is changed.

Transmitter masts amplify outgoing signals from radio stations.

Transistor radio

Radio signals are picked up by the aerials of individual radios. The radio's tuner enables the radio to receive just one radio wave frequency (or radio channel). An amplifier, made up of one or more transistors, boosts the signal carried by the wave and sends it to the speaker. Static is caused by unwanted electrical signals.

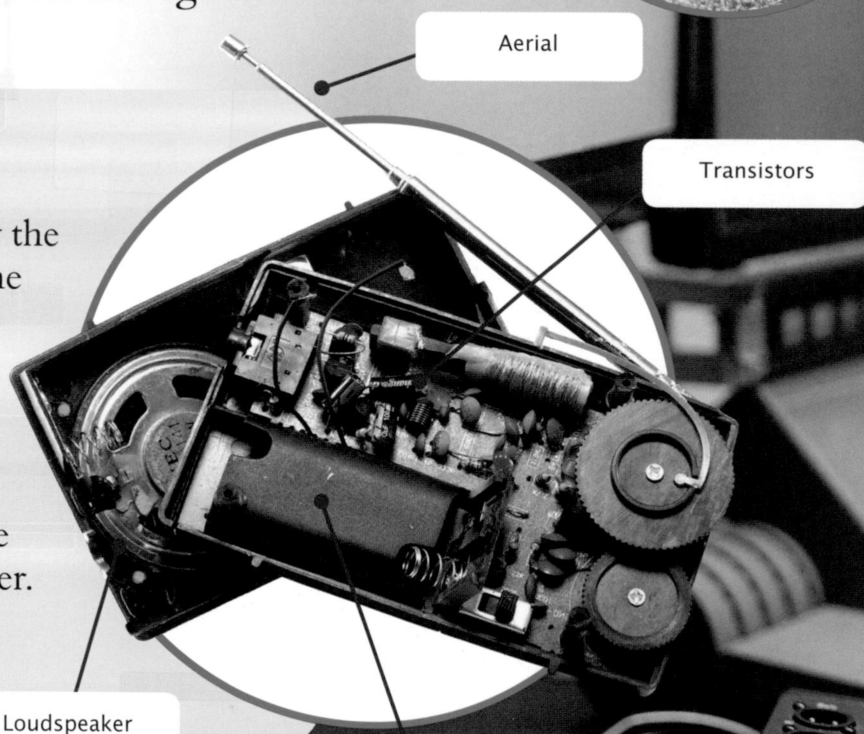
Aerial
Transistors
Loudspeaker
Battery

INVENTOR

Inventor: Guglielmo Marconi

Invention: Radio

Date: 1895

The story: Italian inventor Guglielmo Marconi sent and received the first radio signals. His experiments stretched the distance that wireless communication could travel. In 1901 he successfully received a transmission in Canada from the United Kingdom. This helped to establish a transatlantic radio service.

DID YOU KNOW? There are over 33,000 radio stations around the world.

The microphone can be moved to different positions.
The microphone converts the DJ's voice into electrical signals, which are then transmitted as radio waves.
The headphones let the DJ listen to the music and find tracks while other tunes are playing.
Speaker
The mixing desk enables the DJ to fade different sounds in and out, such as songs, people's voices, jingles, and adverts.
Tuner
TUNING
VOLUME
ON
MAX

Tuner

A radio's antenna, or aerial, receives thousands of radio waves all the time. The tuner separates one wave from all the rest, using a principle called resonance. The tuner resonates at, and amplifies, one particular frequency and ignores all the others.

Remote Controls

The first wireless remote controls used ultrasound (high-pitched sound) to change the channel and volume. When the user pushed a button on the remote control, it clicked and struck a bar inside. Each bar produced a sound at a different frequency, identified by a receiver in the television. There were problems with the ultrasonic remote. Dogs and some humans could hear the piercing signal and the receiver could be triggered by natural occurring noises.

Infrared remotes

Infrared remotes use a light-emitting diode (LED) to transmit signals. Pulses of invisible infrared light carry signals to the electrical device it controls. The device needs to be in the line of sight for the LED to work. Infrared remotes have a range of about 9m (30ft). The signal carries binary code to represent commands such as “power on” and “volume down.”

It is possible to control electrical devices in a smart house from anywhere in the world using an app on a smartphone.

Radio frequency remotes

Radio frequency remotes have a greater range than infrared remotes. They can work at distances of about 30m (100ft) or more. They are useful for opening and closing garages, locking and unlocking cars, and setting car alarms. They transmit at specific frequencies to reduce interference from other radio waves.

INVENTOR

Inventor: Nikola Tesla

Invention: Remote-controlled boat

Date: 1889

The story: Serbian-American inventor Nikola Tesla used radio waves to control the motor in a small boat. He unveiled his remote-controlled boat as part of the electricity exhibition at Madison Square Garden. The crowd thought it was magic because very little was known about radio waves in those days.

DID YOU KNOW? The New Horizon space probe uses remote-control technology to explore beyond our solar system.

A detector in the TV picks up the signal and carries out the encoded instruction.
When you press a button, a beam of infrared light goes to the TV.
Buttons
Circuit board
Shell
LED

Remote-control Cars

A remote-controlled car can be controlled from a distance using a radio transmitter. The transmitter sends a command signal carried by radio waves to a receiver in the car. The signal activates motors inside the car, making it start or stop, or causing its wheels to turn. The car can be powered by batteries or fuel.

The transmitter has its own power source, usually a battery, and sends signals on a frequency that the car is tuned to receive.

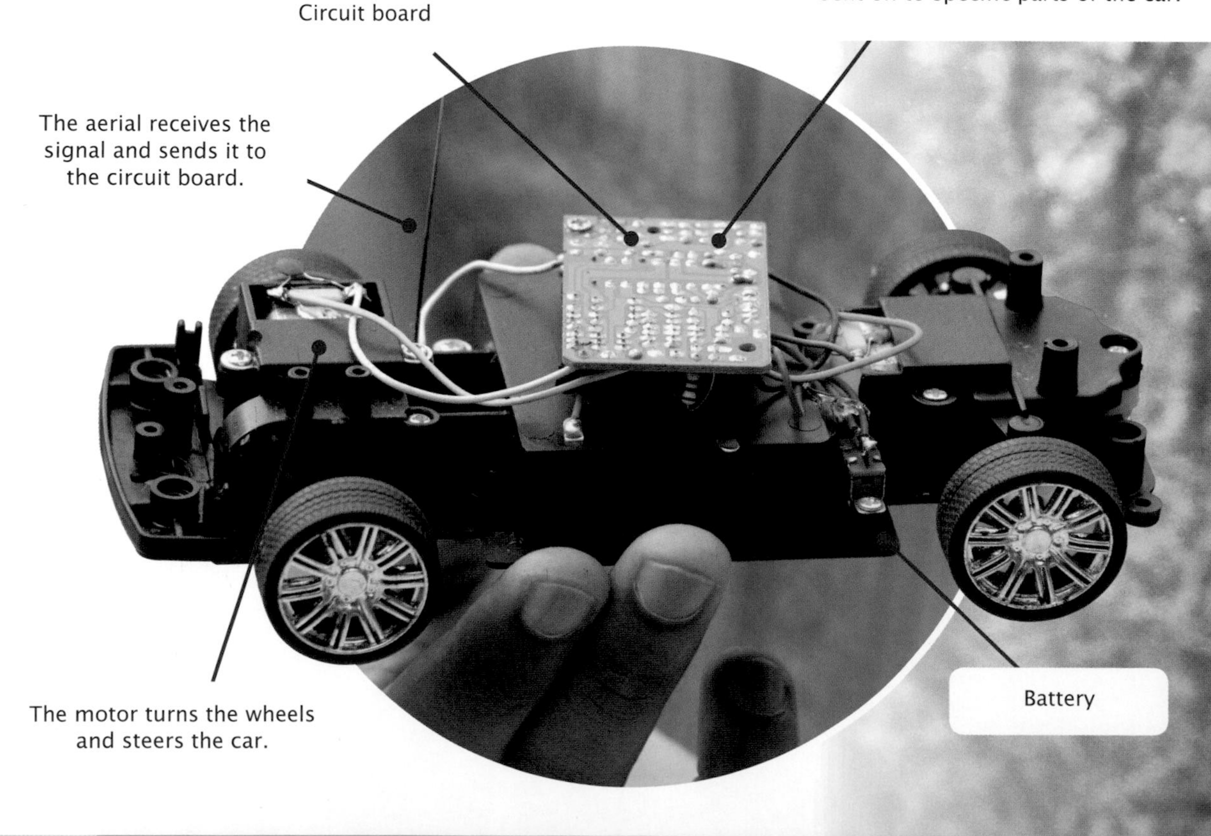
All the command signals are received by the circuit board and sent on to specific parts of the car.
Circuit board
The aerial receives the signal and sends it to the circuit board.
The motor turns the wheels and steers the car.
Battery

DID YOU KNOW? The first radio-controlled car was a miniature Ferrari, which went on sale in 1966.

Engine and fuel

In a fuel-driven, remote-controlled car, the fuel is a mixture of nitromethane and methanol. A blend of castor oil and synthetic oil is added to the fuel to provide lubrication and cooling. The engine works the same way as in a regular-sized car.

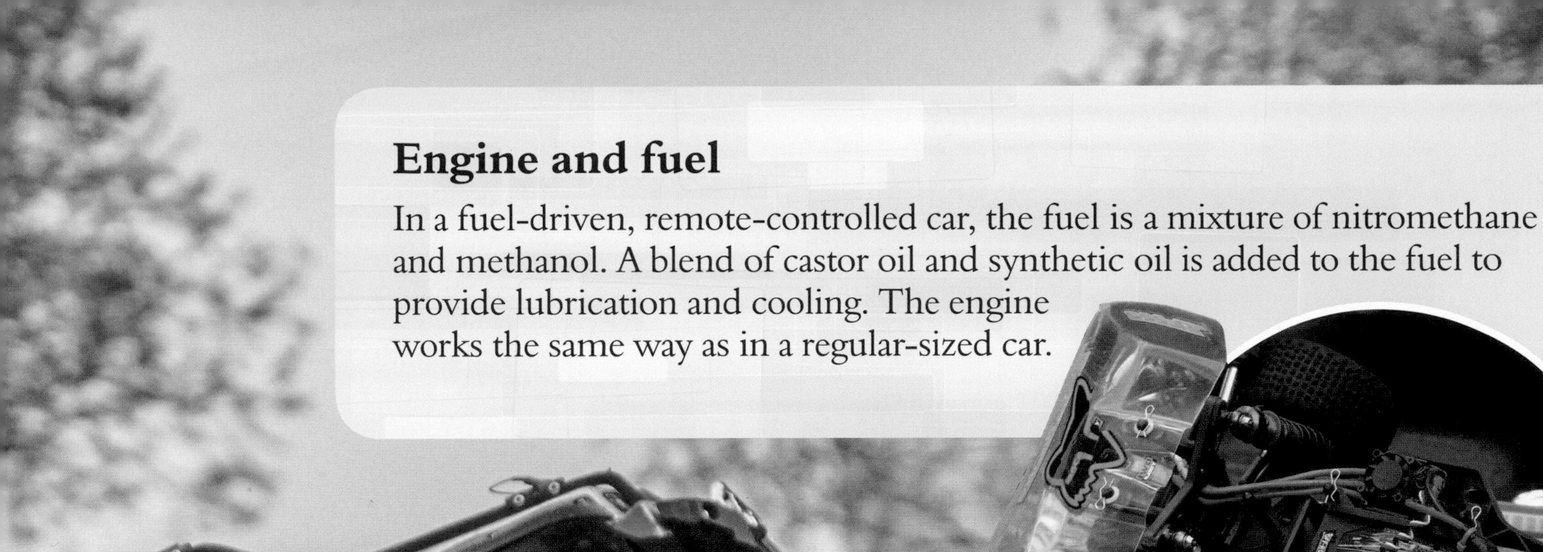

The battery and the circuit board (for receiving commands) are inside the shell of the car, along with the engine and fuel tank.

In 1997, NASA's Sojourner rover became the first radio-controlled vehicle to drive on Mars.

INVENTOR

Inventor: John Hays Hammond, Jr.

Invention: Radio-guided torpedo

Date: 1914

The story: American inventor John Hays Hammond, Jr. is known as "the father of radio control." He invented a target-seeking system, which enabled a remote-controlled ship to locate an enemy ship's searchlights.

Television

Many of today's high-definition, flat-screen televisions use LEDs or "light-emitting diodes." The screens are made up of millions of tiny picture elements called pixels, which can be switched on or off to make a picture.

Behind every LED screen is a bright light. When an electric charge is applied to the liquid crystal inside each pixel, it changes its orientation, either blocking or admitting the light.

LED and OLED televisions

In the case of LED televisions, each pixel is made up of three smaller red, green, and blue sub-pixels. These can be turned on and off very rapidly by liquid crystals, which are like microscopic light switches, to make a moving colour picture.

OLED (organic light-emitting diode) televisions are composed of a layer of organic molecules placed between two electrodes. They do not need a backlight which means they can be thinner and lighter than LED televisions. The contrast between colours is also better, with deeper blacks and brighter whites.

In old TVs, beams of electrons, steered by electromagnets, struck a layer of phosphor on the screen, making spots of light and creating a picture.

INVENTOR

Inventor: George H. Heilmeier

Invention: Liquid-crystal displays (LCD)

Date: 1968

The story: American engineer George H. Heilmeier discovered electro-optic effects in liquid crystals. He showed how they could be manipulated by the application of an electric charge. This led to the development of the first liquid-crystal displays for calculators, watches, and televisions.

DID YOU KNOW? Smart windows use LCD technology to switch from opaque to transparent at the push of a button.

Transmission

TV signals are carried to individual televisions by radio waves from powerful antennae, or sent through underground cable, or beamed as microwaves up to satellites in space and back to Earth. The television turns the signals back into pictures.

Video Games

To make a video game, computer programmers must first write the software—millions of lines of code (computer language instructions) to create the game's storylines and characters. The coding must allow for all possible choices that players can make in the game. Once coding is complete, the game is tested to fix any bugs (errors) before it is released to the public.

Headphones with built-in microphones let players talk to each other anywhere in the world.

Games consoles

A console is a highly specialized computer. It has an operating system to organize and control the hardware and software. It also has RAM (random-access memory) to store a game as it's played, providing the necessary speed for an interactive gaming experience.

Portable game consoles

Today's portable game consoles, such as the Nintendo Switch®, feature more immersive player experiences. They contain devices such as accelerometers (to measure acceleration) and gyroscopes (to measure tilting motion) in order to track the player's movements and gestures. Some also contain a "haptic feedback" system to give the player the sense of touching objects in the game.

INVENTION

Inventor: Ralph Baer

Invention: First games console

Date: 1969

The story: German-born American inventor Ralph Baer was inspired by watching television to investigate how to play games on TV. The result was the "Brown Box," a prototype for the first multiplayer, multiprogram video game system.

The first video game was called Pong. It was played like tennis, with two lines for bats and a dot for the ball, which bounced around the screen. The aim was to stop the ball passing beyond your bat.

A controller is needed to play the games.

DID YOU KNOW? In the original arcade version of Donkey Kong, Mario was called Jumpman and was a carpenter, not a plumber.

Virtual Reality

Virtual reality (VR) is a 3D, computer-generated environment. People can explore and interact with the environment by using a headset or gloves fitted with sensors. To create a truly immersive experience, the VR system needs to give users a minimum 100-degree field of view. They also need a frame rate of around 60 frames per second for the VR world to be convincing—humans perceive anything higher than 12 frames per second as motion.

Eye and head tracking

The VR system tracks the movements of the viewer's eyes and head using an accelerometer, a gyroscope, and a magnetometer (to identify their position relative to Earth's magnetic field). The computer absorbs this data and shifts the picture as the user looks around.

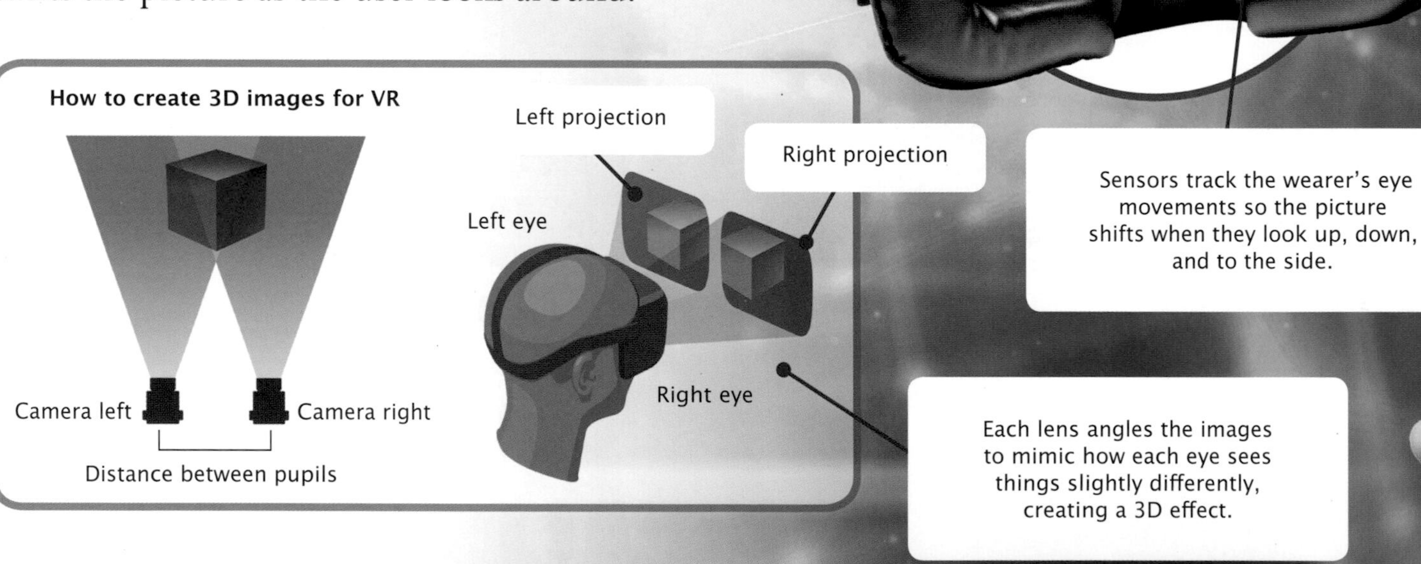

How to create 3D images for VR
Camera left
Camera right
Distance between pupils
Left projection
Right projection
Left eye
Right eye
Sensors track the wearer's eye movements so the picture shifts when they look up, down, and to the side.
Each lens angles the images to mimic how each eye sees things slightly differently, creating a 3D effect.

INVENTION

Inventor: Timoni West

Invention: Virtual Reality developing

Date: 2018

The story: Virtual-reality designer Timoni West works in Unity, a 3D game engine that lets developers code and design in one environment, then import their app or game to over 30 platforms. She is working on a project to enable developers to build games inside virtual reality itself.

The helmet lets
the wearer
manipulate virtual
objects and
perform actions in
a virtual world.

Virtual-reality glove

A special VR glove lets the wearer "touch" virtual objects. The glove has internal "tendons" that tense and relax to simulate the wearer's sense of touch.

DID YOU KNOW? In 2015, Marriot hotels used virtual reality for customers to view hotels they may like to visit. Headsets transported people from London to Maui instantly.

Cameras

When the button is pressed on a digital camera, an aperture (hole) briefly opens at the front, letting light enter through the lens. An electronic light sensor captures the image and breaks it into millions of tiny picture elements called pixels. The sensor measures the colour and brightness of each pixel and stores it as a number.

The shutter lets light through to the sensor.

Shutter

The shutter is the mechanism that opens and closes the aperture. A slow shutter speed lets in more light, resulting in a brighter image, but objects in motion will appear blurry.

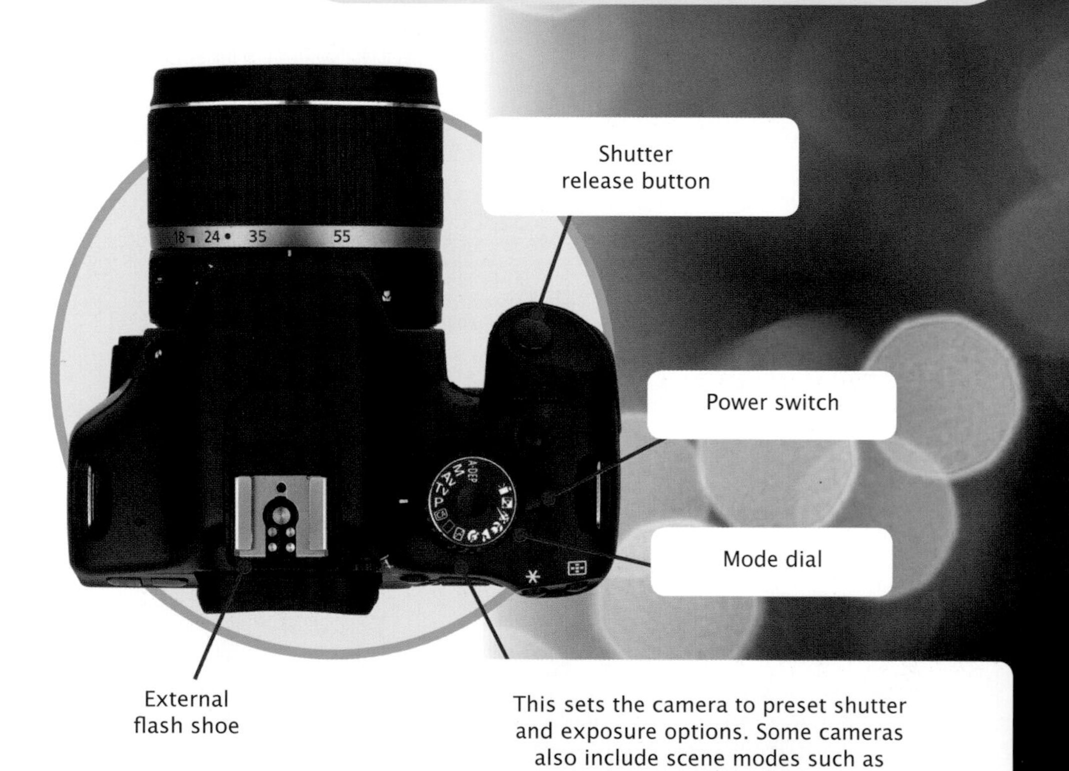
18 24 35 55

Shutter release button

Power switch

Mode dial

This sets the camera to preset shutter and exposure options. Some cameras also include scene modes such as landscape, portrait and sports.

External flash shoe

Flexible photos

Digital photos can be adjusted in an image editing program. To make an image 10 percent brighter, the program increases the number representing brightness in each pixel by 10 percent.

DID YOU KNOW? The Apollo 11 moon mission left 12 cameras behind on the moon.

The menu button lets the user navigate the camera's set-up options.
Information button
Viewfinder
Zoom in
Automatic exposure and automatic focus lock
Zoom out
Image playback button
Delete button
The LCD screen lets the user adjust the shot before they take the photograph.
The selection pad lets the user scroll through the setting options and the photographs.

INVENTOR

Inventor: Steven Sasson

Invention: First digital camera

Date: 1976

The story: American electrical engineer Steven Sasson designed a prototype digital camera. His bosses at Kodak were not impressed. Sasson said, "They were convinced no one would ever want to look at their pictures on a television."

Smartphones and Tablets

Smartphones and tablets are mobile computers, with operating systems that run software programs called apps. They are powered by a rechargeable battery, and contain accelerometers and gyroscopes that can sense the device's orientation, so the screen image turns to allow for better viewing.

The gallery contains all the user's photographs, videos, and screenshots.

Touchscreen

The screen of a smartphone or tablet has a transparent layer of material that stores an electrical charge. When a finger touches it, sensors detect the change in electric current and its location, and the software commands an action to be performed.

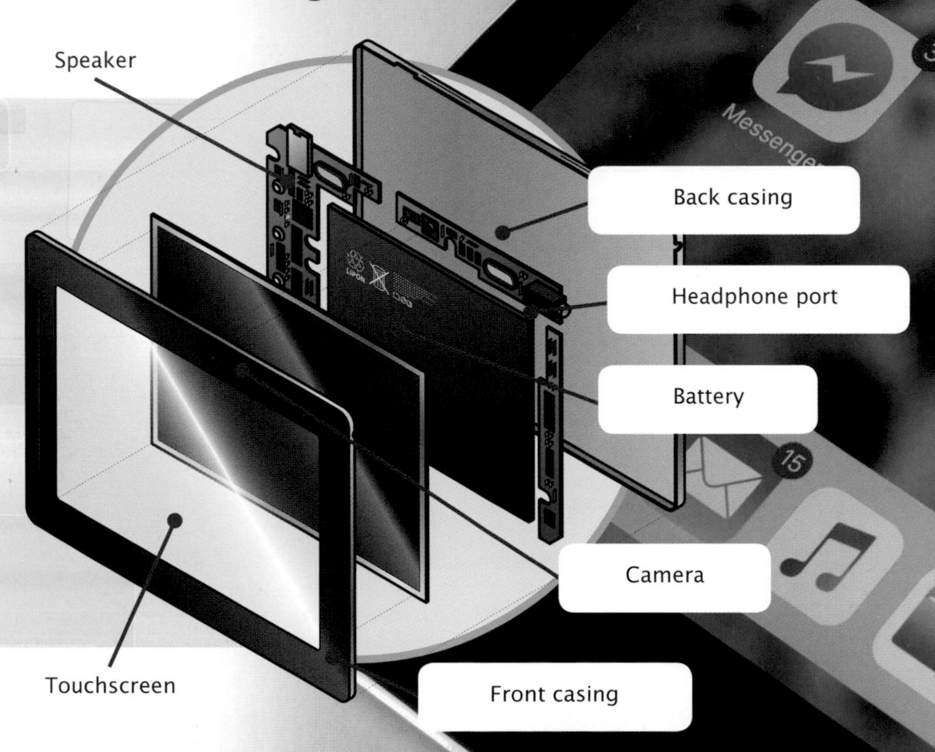

Speaker
Back casing
Headphone port
Battery
Camera
Touchscreen
Front casing

INVENTION

Inventor: Martin Cooper

Invention: Handheld portable phone

Date: 1973

The story: American telecommunications developer Martin Cooper helped to produce the first handheld portable phone. The prototype was named *DynaTAC*. It was about the size and weight of a house brick and was shaped like a shoe.

DID YOU KNOW? Nikola Tesla predicted the invention of smartphones in 1926.

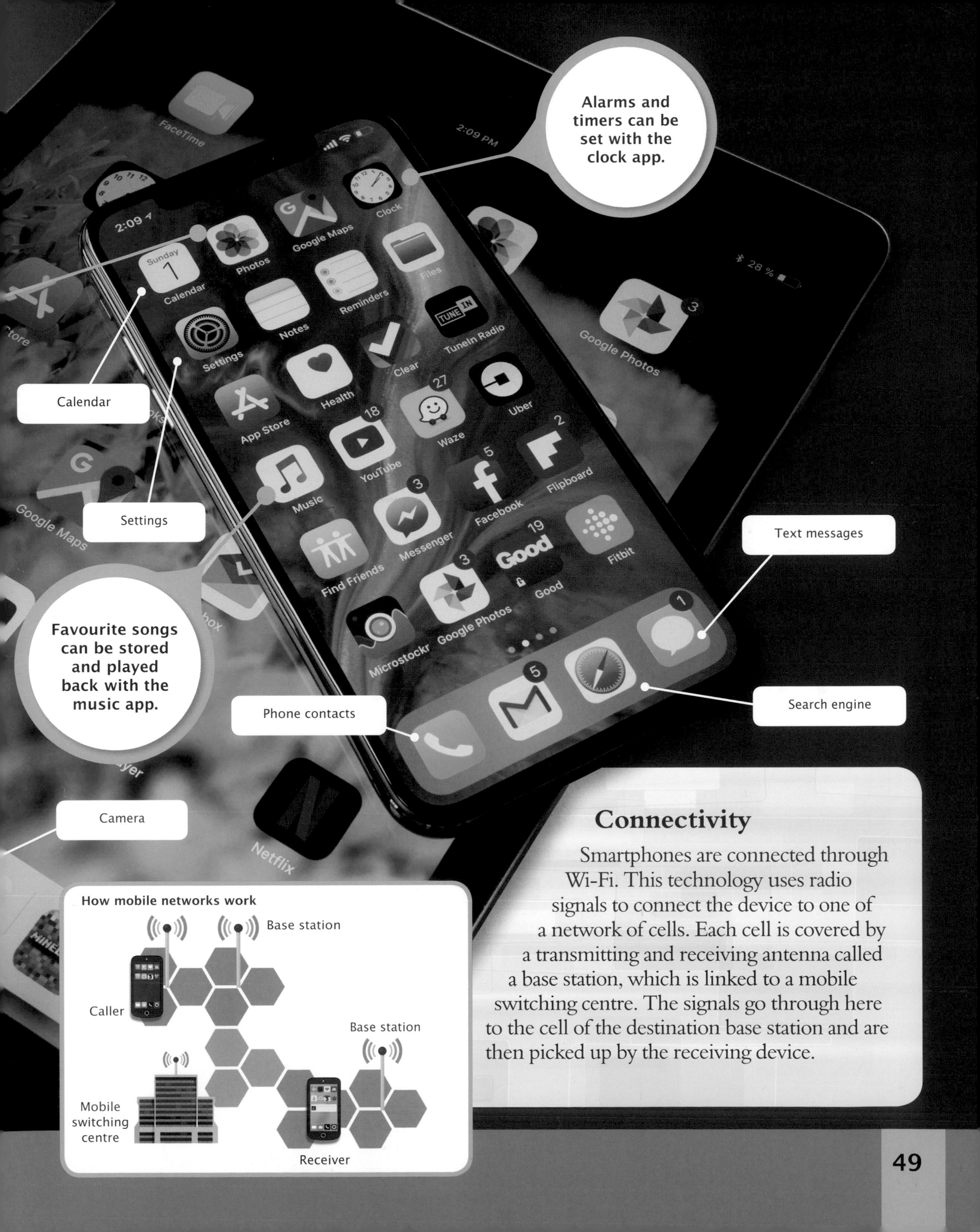
Alarms and timers can be set with the clock app.
Calendar
Settings
Favourite songs can be stored and played back with the music app.
Phone contacts
Text messages
Search engine
Camera
How mobile networks work
Base station
Caller
Base station
Mobile switching centre
Receiver

Connectivity

Smartphones are connected through Wi-Fi. This technology uses radio signals to connect the device to one of a network of cells. Each cell is covered by a transmitting and receiving antenna called a base station, which is linked to a mobile switching centre. The signals go through here to the cell of the destination base station and are then picked up by the receiving device.

Watches

Inside a quartz watch, a battery sends electricity to a quartz crystal, causing it to vibrate at a precise frequency. An electronic circuit converts the vibrations into electric pulses, one per second. These can power a digital display or drive a small electric motor that makes the watch's hands turn.

Quartz is piezoelectric—it converts electricity into motion. When electricity is passed through a quartz crystal, it vibrates exactly 32,768 times a second.
Alarm button
Date
Light button
Settings button
N
E
W
S
11-2 FRI
7:58
14

Digital watches

Digital watches show the time using a liquid-crystal display (LCD). A computer in the watch tells it to reset back to 1:00:00 once it reaches 12:59:59.

Wheels
Jewels
Gears
Springs

Mechanical watch

The inside of a mechanical watch is known as the movement. It has wheels and gears to move hour, minute, and second hands around the watch face. Small jewels are used to reduce friction and help the gears move smoothly. The watches don't need electricity because they are powered by a spring, called a mainspring, which must be wound for the watch to work.

DID YOU KNOW? The Rolex Deepsea Challenge® watch was submerged 10,908 m (35,787 ft) and continued to work.

Minute hand
The spring turns the gear wheel to move the minute hand. Another gear turns the hour hand.
Smartwatches are powered by rechargeable batteries. They are charged by connecting them to a mains socket with a USB lead and plug.
Hour hand
Date
Weather
Email
Music
Phone contacts
Settings button
Time
Charging port

INVENTION

Inventor: Peter Henlein

Invention: Pomander watch

Date: 1510

The story: German locksmith and clockmaker Peter Henlein created the first small, spring-powered brass watches. He replaced the pendulum with a spring mechanism. They were designed to be worn as a necklace.

Microchips

Microchips are the brains of all electronic devices. They are integrated circuits etched onto a silicon wafer. Silicon is used because it can either conduct or contain electricity. The circuits (transistors and wiring built onto the chip) convert electrical signals into data in the form of on-off pulses. This is represented in binary as 0 (off) and 1 (on). Each binary number is a bit. A group of eight bits is a byte. Data is stored on microchips in bytes.

Microchips can be very small.
Two rows of pins connect the microchip to the circuit board and conduct electronic signals.
The electronic parts are protected by a plastic case.
A single chip can contain thousands of transistors.

Microprocessor

A microprocessor is a microchip that has all the functions of the central processing unit of a computer. It can perform operations, move data, and make decisions.

DID YOU KNOW? Scientists are working on producing microchips the size of molecules.

INVENTOR
Inventor: Jeri Ellsworth
Invention: Retro gaming joystick
Date: 2004
The story: Video game developer Jeri Ellsworth taught herself chip design. She created a joystick, which contained a microchip with 30 retro video games on it. It was a hit with game players.
Silicon is manufactured as long crystals, which are then sliced into thin discs known as wafers.
The wafers are heated and coated in silicon dioxide, then exposed to ultraviolet light to add a hard, protective layer.
Electronic circuits are etched on the wafer by adding chemicals to change the composition of certain parts of the surface.

Home Computers

A computer is essentially an information processor. First, it receives data as inputs from, for example, a keyboard, mouse, or scanner. The data is worked on by its central processing unit according to programmed instructions. Finally, it outputs the data via a monitor, printer, or speaker.

Central processing unit

The computer's "brain" is called the central processing unit, or CPU. The CPU is a chip containing millions of transistors—each ransistor is like an individual brain cell. The CPU executes stored instructions and performs calculations.

The buttons on the mouse perform different functions, depending on what program is being used.

The mouse mat lets the mouse move smoothly.

The mouse controls the position of the curser on the screen. The mouse is controlled either by an infrared laser or a red LED, which projects light onto the mouse mat.

INVENTOR

Inventor: Steve Wozniak

Invention: Apple I

Date: 1976

The story: American inventor Steve Wozniak co-founded the computer company Apple. He designed and made the first affordable home computer with easily obtained resources. It was a typewriter-like keyboard connected to a TV, called the *Apple I*.

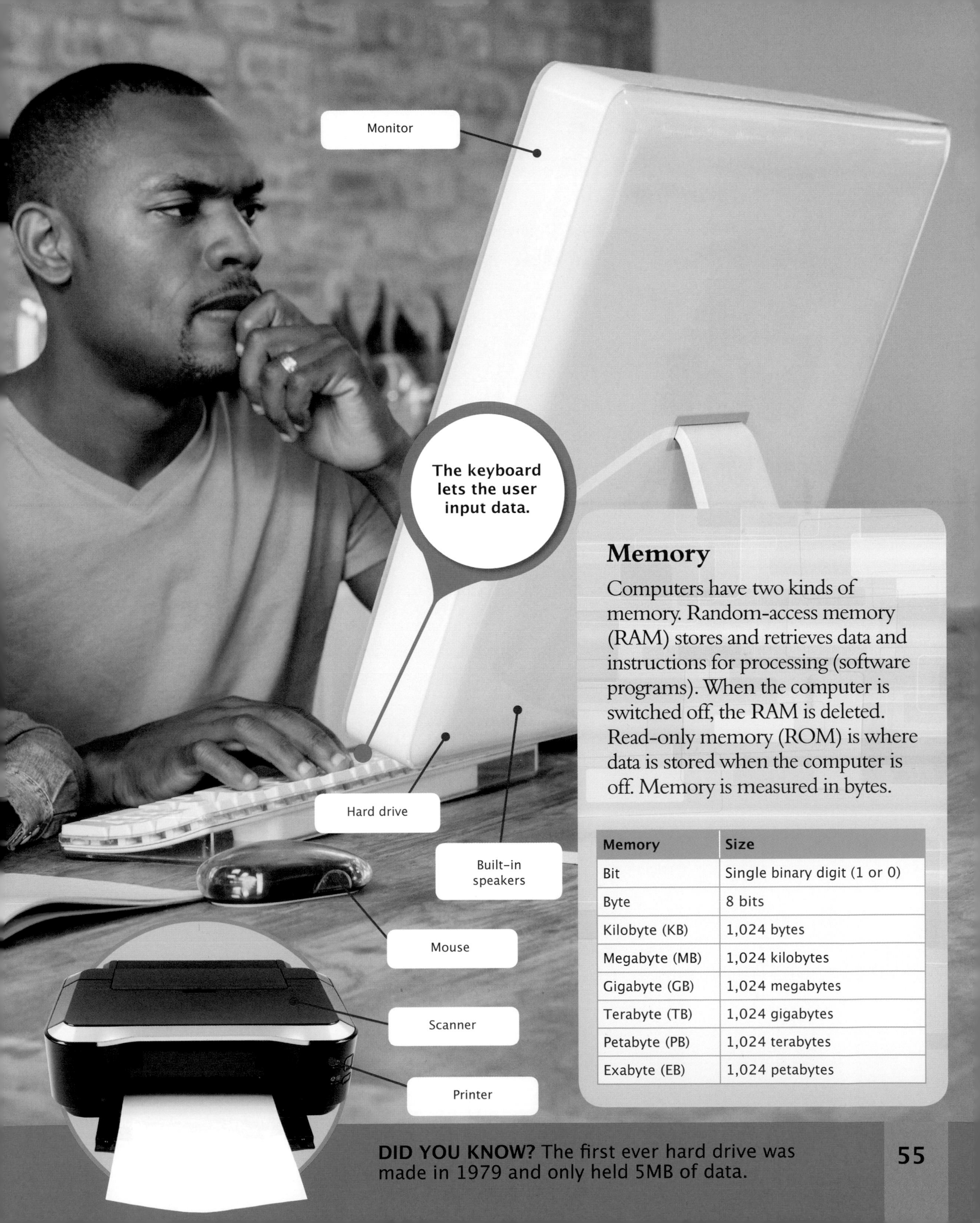
Monitor
The keyboard lets the user input data.
Hard drive
Built-in speakers
Mouse
Scanner
Printer

Memory

Computers have two kinds of memory. Random-access memory (RAM) stores and retrieves data and instructions for processing (software programs). When the computer is switched off, the RAM is deleted. Read-only memory (ROM) is where data is stored when the computer is off. Memory is measured in bytes.

Memory	Size
Bit	Single binary digit (1 or 0)
Byte	8 bits
Kilobyte (KB)	1,024 bytes
Megabyte (MB)	1,024 kilobytes
Gigabyte (GB)	1,024 megabytes
Terabyte (TB)	1,024 gigabytes
Petabyte (PB)	1,024 terabytes
Exabyte (EB)	1,024 petabytes

DID YOU KNOW? The first ever hard drive was made in 1979 and only held 5MB of data.

The Internet

The Internet—short for "interconnected network"—is a global network of computers, enabling communication, data transfer, and information sharing. Computers can connect through various kinds of hardware, including routers, servers, mobile phone masts, and satellites, linked by cables, or wirelessly by radio signals. For the Internet to work, it also needs protocols, which are common sets of rules that enable computers to understand each other.

World Wide Web (WWW)

The WWW is a network of websites that use the Internet. It works thanks to two protocols: HTTP (HyperText Transfer Protocol) enables computers to communicate and swap files over the Internet. HTML (HyperText Markup Language) enables computers to understand the files they receive so they can display them correctly.

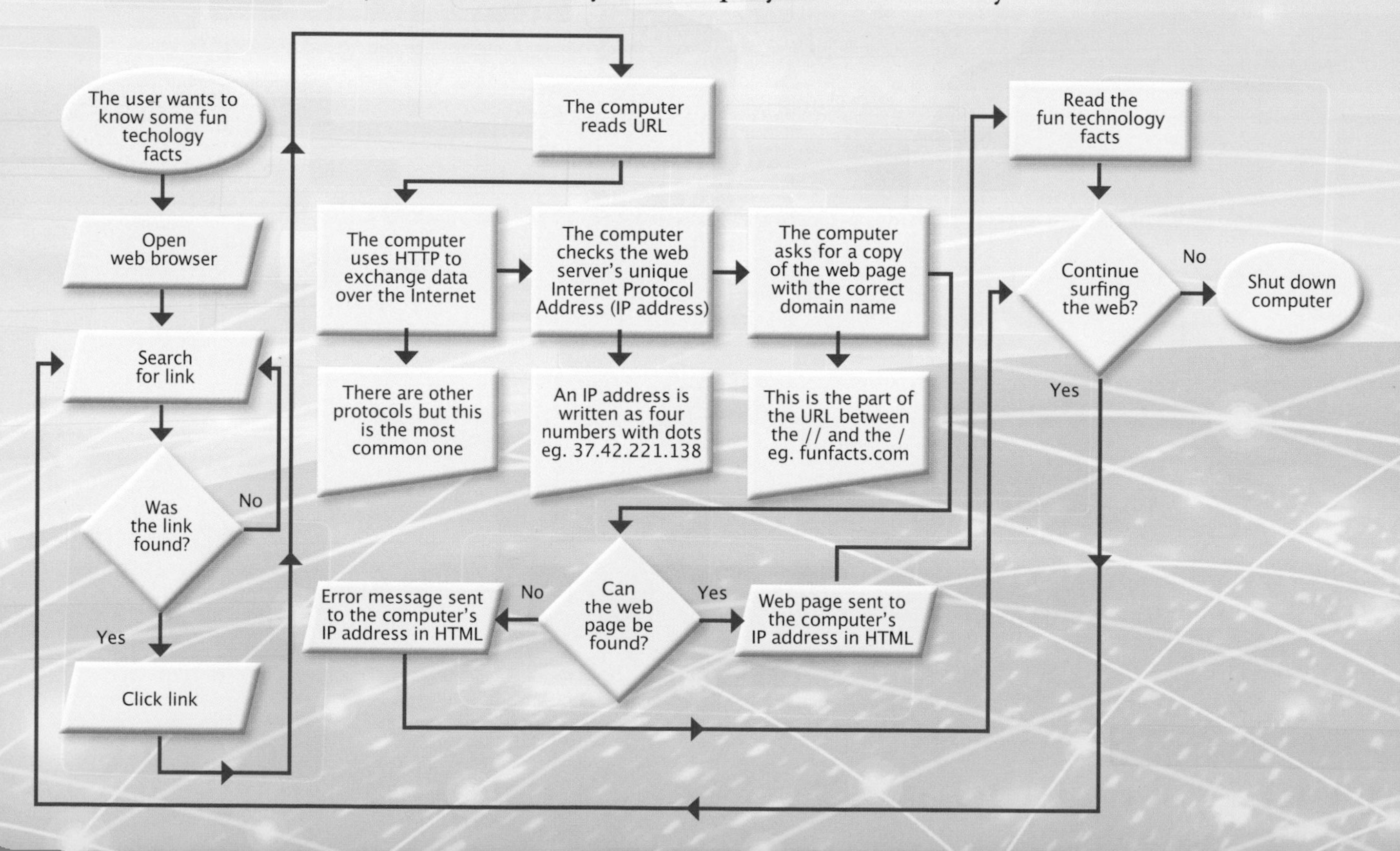

The user wants to know some fun techology facts
Open web browser
Search for link
Was the link found?
No
Yes
Click link
The computer reads URL
The computer uses HTTP to exchange data over the Internet
There are other protocols but this is the most common one
The computer checks the web server's unique Internet Protocol Address (IP address)
An IP address is written as four numbers with dots eg. 37.42.221.138
The computer asks for a copy of the web page with the correct domain name
This is the part of the URL between the // and the / eg. funfacts.com
Can the web page be found?
No
Error message sent to the computer's IP address in HTML
Yes
Web page sent to the computer's IP address in HTML
Read the fun technology facts
Continue surfing the web?
No
Shut down computer
Yes

DID YOU KNOW? The first email was sent in 1971 by American programmer Ray Tomlinson.

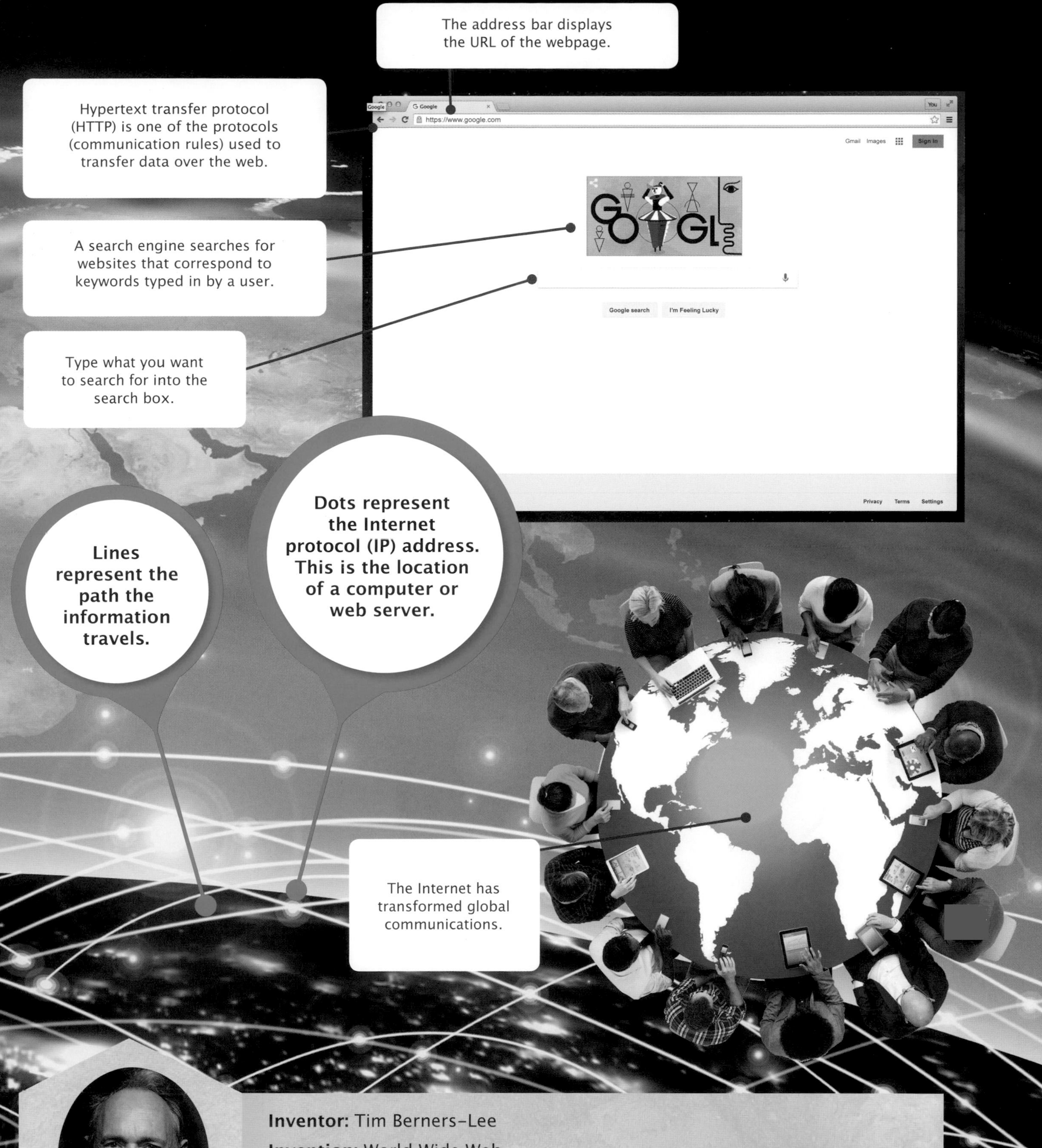
The address bar displays the URL of the webpage.
Hypertext transfer protocol (HTTP) is one of the protocols (communication rules) used to transfer data over the web.
A search engine searches for websites that correspond to keywords typed in by a user.
Type what you want to search for into the search box.
https://www.google.com
Google search
I'm Feeling Lucky
Lines represent the path the information travels.
Dots represent the Internet protocol (IP) address. This is the location of a computer or web server.
The Internet has transformed global communications.

INVENTOR

Inventor: Tim Berners-Lee

Invention: World Wide Web

Date: 1989

The story: British software engineer Tim Berners-Lee created the World Wide Web for scientists to easily share data about their experiments. He had his big idea in 1989, and the following year he wrote the software that enabled this to happen.

Cloud Storage

Cloud storage is a method of saving data to a vast, remote network of powerful computers, known as the "cloud," which is accessed via the Internet. This is a safe, convenient, and flexible way of storing data, compared to storing it on a computer hard drive or memory stick.

Virtualization

Data is stored on large computers called servers. To store so much data, the cloud uses "virtualization": servers are subdivided into several smaller "virtual machines," each running their own operating system. Virtualization reduces the need for too many physical machines.

Websites such as Flickr and Google Photos host online photo albums to store, share, and back up digital photographs.

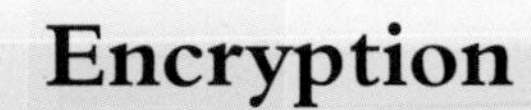

Encryption

Data in the cloud is kept secure through encryption (conversion into a code). Every computer owns two unique encryption keys, one public, one private, linked to one another. The public key is given to any computer that wants to send a file. The encrypted file can then only be decrypted by the destination computer.

Information placed in the cloud is stored in enormous database servers.

For security, cloud providers store data in multiple locations.

INVENTOR

Inventor: J. C. R. Licklider

Invention: The cloud

Date: 1962

The story: In the early 1960s, American computer scientist J. C. R. Licklider was one of the first to suggest the creation of a global network of computers. His ideas led to the development of the Internet and cloud storage.

Favourite albums and songs can be stored and accessed remotely from anywhere at any time.
Movies can be watched directly from the servers of online providers without downloading them to a device.
Social networking sites such as Facebook, Twitter, and Instagram enable members to post videos and pictures. All the data is stored on their servers.
E-books and audio books are stored on the provider's servers and downloaded when the user wants to read or listen to them.
Web email providers such as Gmail and Hotmail have the option to store messages on their own servers.
Millions of video files are uploaded, stored, and streamed on YouTube.

DID YOU KNOW? It is possible to edit documents in the cloud using different apps.

Wi-Fi

Wi-Fi is a technology that uses radio waves to transmit information wirelessly across a network. A computer's wireless adapter converts data into a radio signal, which it transmits via an antenna to a router. The router converts it back into data to be sent to the Internet through an Ethernet cable. The system also works in reverse. Multiple devices can link to the same Wi-Fi network through a single router.

Living room
Dining room
Bedroom
Nursery
Bathroom
Kitchen
Fire alarms
Heating
Music
Lights
Water temperature
Energy
Security cameras
Wi-Fi connected devices can be controlled using an app on a smartphone or tablet.

DID YOU KNOW? Wi-Fi doesn't actually stand for anything. It's not short for "Wireless Fidelity," which is a made-up term and means nothing.

INVENTOR

Inventor: John O'Sullivan

Invention: Wireless connectivity

Date: 1990

The story: Australian electrical engineer John O'Sullivan and his team created microchips for wireless connection. The microchips slowed down the signal transmission speeds by splitting the signals into smaller components and then recombining them at the receiver.

WLAN

A Wi-Fi network, also known as a Wireless Local Area Network (WLAN), can be any limited area, such as a home, school, or office building. All electronic devices can be connected to the WLAN. Users can move around within the network and still be connected.

Lights can be turned on and off in any room in the house and their brightness altered.

The preferred settings of the water temperature for each person can be easily saved.

The garage door can be opened and shut at a push of a button without the driver having to leave the car.

The timer on the cooker can be set and controlled.

Weather Satellites

Weather satellites carry instruments called radiometers, which can detect visible, infrared, or microwave radiation. They scan the Earth to form images, which are digitized and then transmitted to receiving stations on the ground. Meteorologists study and interpret images sent from the satellites. There are two types of weather satellite.

Geostationary satellites

Geostationary satellites hover over the same spot on the Earth's equator by orbiting Earth at the same speed that the Earth turns. They are at an altitude of about 35,000 km (22,500 miles). They scan the same geographical area continuously.

Weather satellite data is transmitted to receiving stations and relayed to weather forecast organizations all over the world.

Polar satellites

Polar satellites orbit the Earth at an altitude of about 805 km (500 miles). They move north to south, passing over both poles during their orbit. Two polar satellites can monitor a location once every six hours.

L
L
L

Data from weather satellites helps meteorologists make short- and long-term weather forecasts.

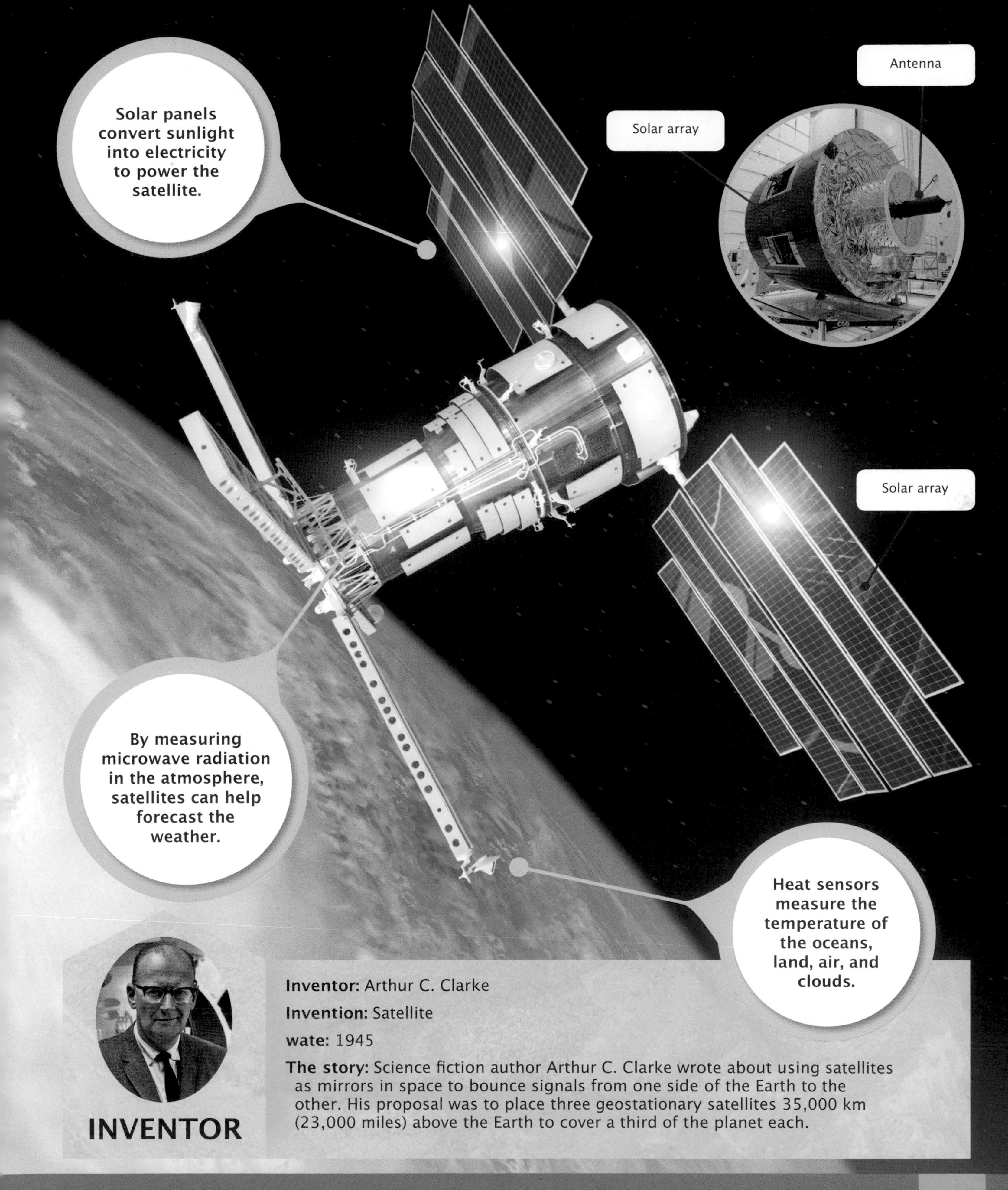
Solar panels convert sunlight into electricity to power the satellite.
Antenna
Solar array
Solar array
By measuring microwave radiation in the atmosphere, satellites can help forecast the weather.
Heat sensors measure the temperature of the oceans, land, air, and clouds.
INVENTOR

Inventor: Arthur C. Clarke

Invention: Satellite

wate: 1945

The story: Science fiction author Arthur C. Clarke wrote about using satellites as mirrors in space to bounce signals from one side of the Earth to the other. His proposal was to place three geostationary satellites 35,000 km (23,000 miles) above the Earth to cover a third of the planet each.

DID YOU KNOW? In October 1957, the Russian spacecraft Sputnik was the first satellite to be launched.

GPS

The global positioning system (GPS) is a worldwide navigation system based in space. It consists of 30 satellites located in 6 orbits around Earth, with 4 operational satellites and a spare satellite in each orbit. A GPS receiver (often called a satnav) on Earth works in conjunction with the satellites to calculate a precise location.

Navigation satellites

There are at least four GPS satellites able to transmit to any point on Earth at all times. Each satellite constantly transmits information about its position and the exact time. These signals travel at the speed of light.

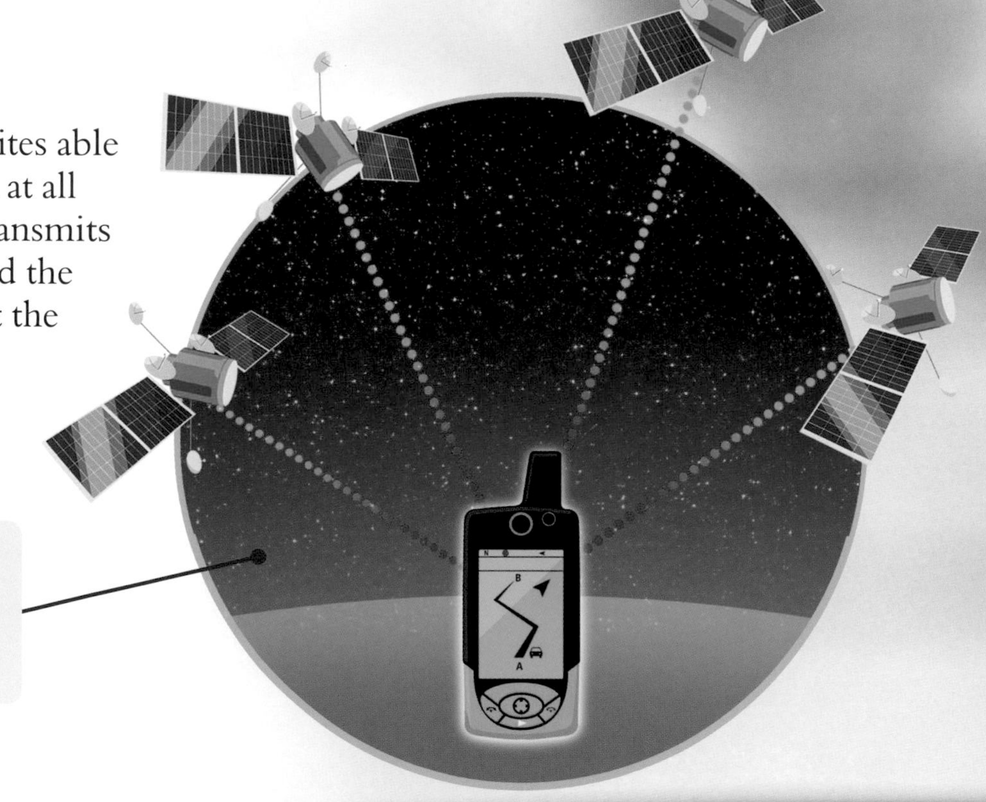

A satnav locates four or more satellites, calculates its distance from each, and uses this information to work out its own location.

INVENTOR

Inventor: Gladys West

Invention: Global positioning calculations

Date: 1950s–1960s

The story: American mathematician Gladys West worked at a US Navy base in Virginia, where she recorded satellite locations and calculated the size and shape of the Earth. Her work contributed to the accuracy of GPS.

DID YOU KNOW? It takes 12 hours for each GPS satellite to orbit the Earth.

Satnav

The satnav calculates how far away a satellite is by measuring the time it takes for the signal to arrive, then uses this to work out its own position. The more satellites it uses, the more accurate the calculation. A satnav comes pre-loaded with maps of the area.

Smartphones and smartwatches have their own GPS. They use this to show the user where he or she is on a map, and also give directions to other locations.

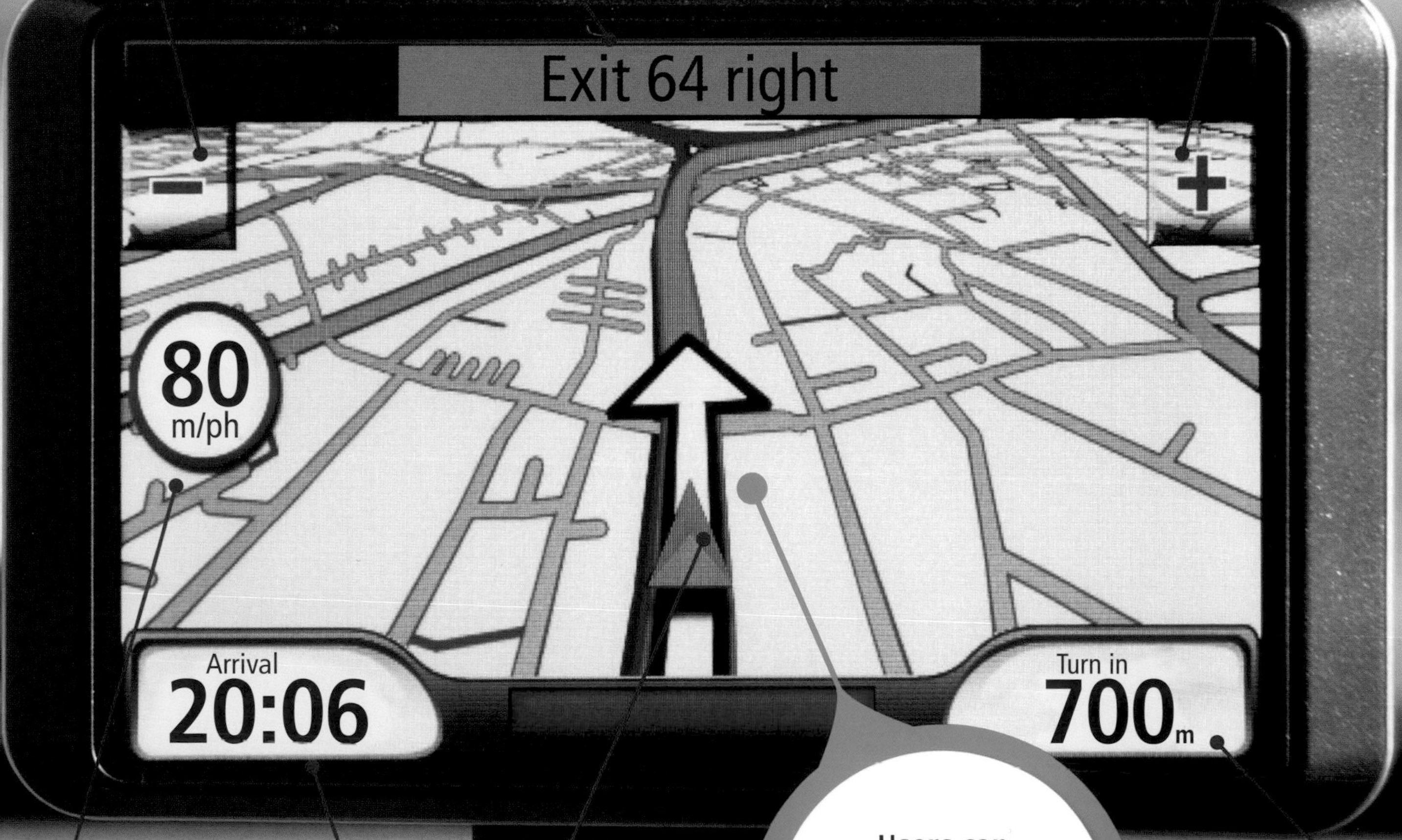

Exit 64 right
80
m/ph
Arrival
20:06
Turn in
700m

Next junction information

Zoom out

Zoom in

Speed limit

Time of arrival

Road travelling on

Distance to next junction

Users can find how to get to a place by inputting the address of the desired destination.

Batteries

A battery contains chemicals that store energy until it is needed. They provide a mobile source of power. Each battery has a positive (+) and negative (–) terminal. When the two terminals are connected with wires to form a circuit, electrons flow from the negative terminal through the device being powered into the positive terminal.

Bulb

Switch

Wire

BATTERY +

Battery

The wires enable the flow of electrons.

A chemical reaction takes place when electrons flow from the negative to the positive terminal to create electrical energy.

Rechargeable batteries

Some batteries are rechargeable. In cars, for example, the engine turns a miniature electric generator called an alternator, which feeds current back into the battery to recharge it. The batteries in phones, tablets, and laptops are rechargeable using electricity from wall plugs. The electrical energy is converted back to chemical energy inside the battery.

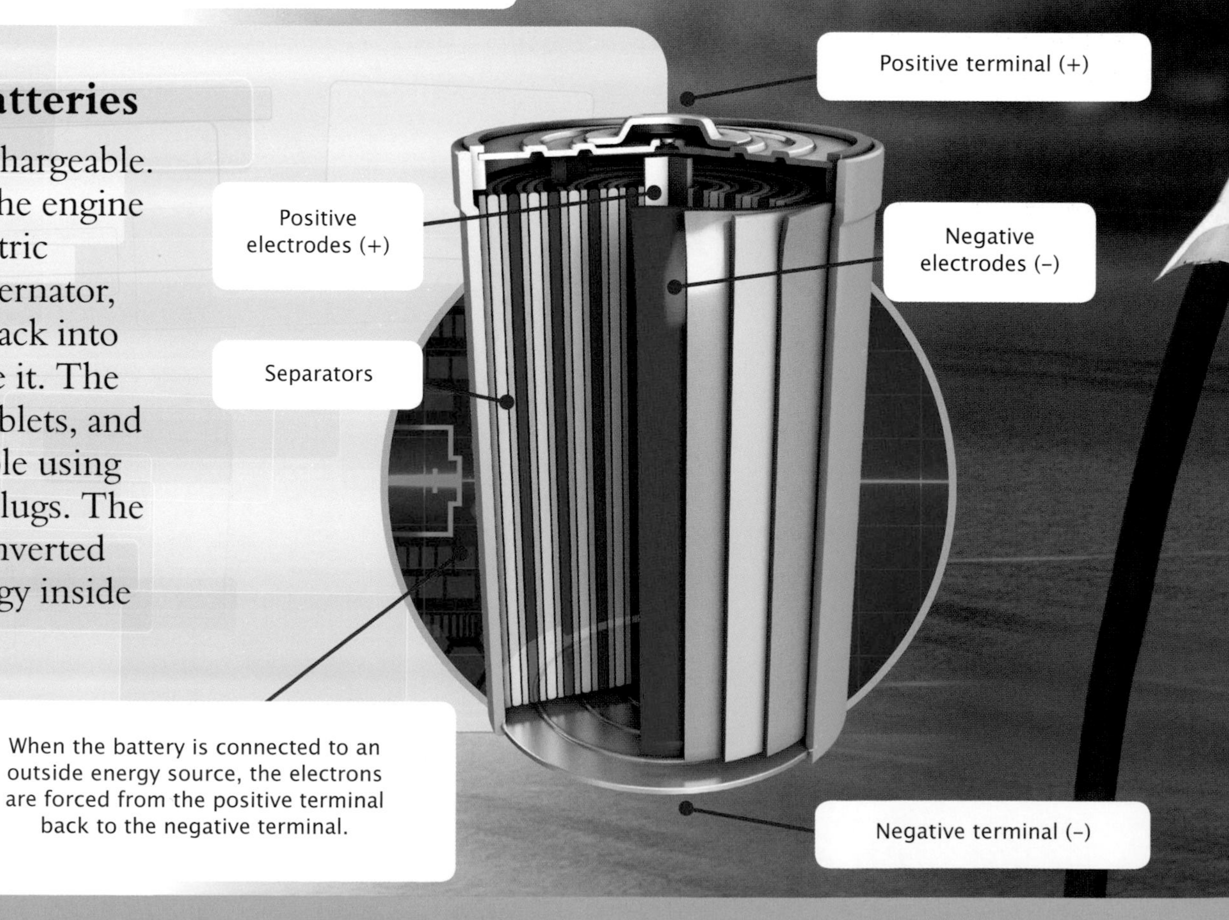
Positive terminal (+)
Positive electrodes (+)
Negative electrodes (–)
Separators
When the battery is connected to an outside energy source, the electrons are forced from the positive terminal back to the negative terminal.
Negative terminal (–)

DID YOU KNOW? Recycling your batteries is better for the environment.

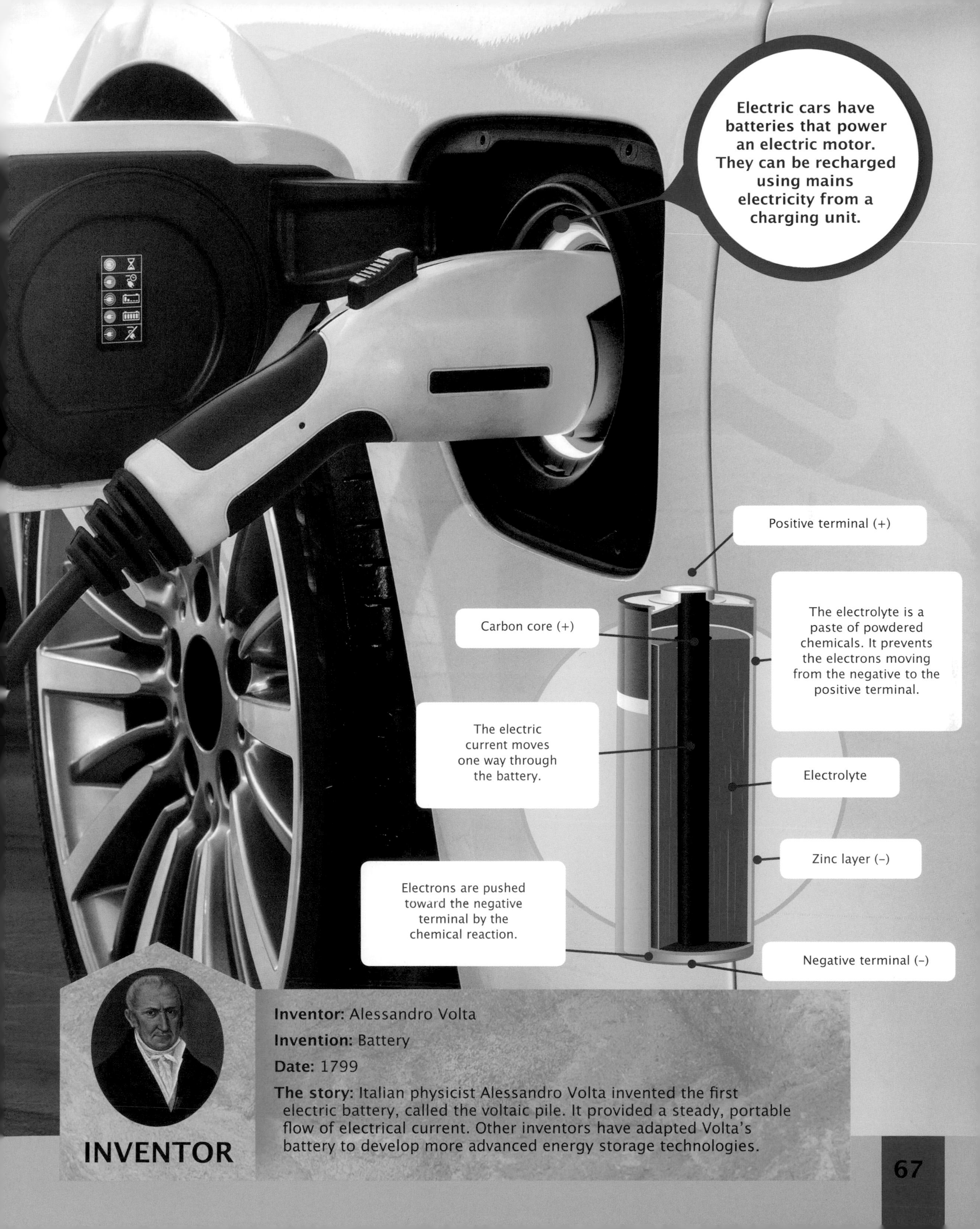
Electric cars have batteries that power an electric motor. They can be recharged using mains electricity from a charging unit.
Positive terminal (+)
Carbon core (+)
The electrolyte is a paste of powdered chemicals. It prevents the electrons moving from the negative to the positive terminal.
The electric current moves one way through the battery.
Electrolyte
Zinc layer (–)
Electrons are pushed toward the negative terminal by the chemical reaction.
Negative terminal (–)

INVENTOR

Inventor: Alessandro Volta

Invention: Battery

Date: 1799

The story: Italian physicist Alessandro Volta invented the first electric battery, called the voltaic pile. It provided a steady, portable flow of electrical current. Other inventors have adapted Volta's battery to develop more advanced energy storage technologies.

Electric Power

Electricity can be generated by burning fossil fuels, such as coal, oil, and gas. It can also be created by harnessing the power of wind, water, and the sun, and through nuclear reactions.

Hydropower

Dams store water in reservoirs. Water released from the reservoir flows through a turbine, making its blades rotate. This creates power in the generator. The mechanical energy is converted into electrical energy.

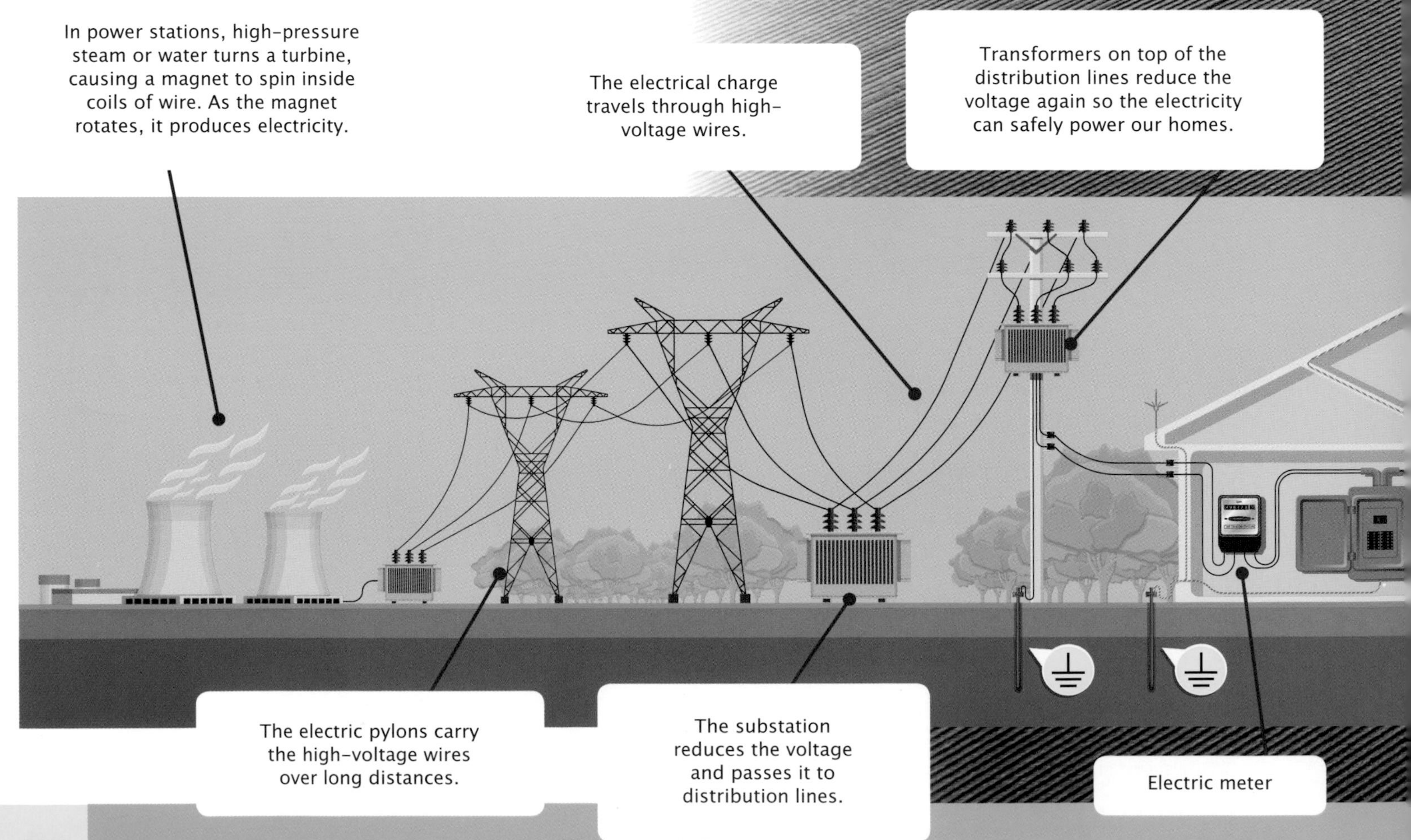
In power stations, high-pressure steam or water turns a turbine, causing a magnet to spin inside coils of wire. As the magnet rotates, it produces electricity.
The electrical charge travels through high-voltage wires.
Transformers on top of the distribution lines reduce the voltage again so the electricity can safely power our homes.
The electric pylons carry the high-voltage wires over long distances.
The substation reduces the voltage and passes it to distribution lines.
Electric meter

INVENTOR
Inventor: Michael Faraday
Invention: Electric generator
Date: 1831
The story: British inventor Michael Faraday invented an electric generator. It had a magnet, which moved inside a coil of copper wire to create an electric current.
Electricity is generated when the wind turns the blades of the wind turbine. The more wind, the more electricity.
Appliances outlets
The symbol for an "earth electrode," which is a pipe or other conductor, partly buried, to conduct electricity safely into the ground.

DID YOU KNOW? The first electric power plant was opened in New York City by Thomas Edison in 1882.

Running Water

The water supplied to our homes starts off as rain. The rain filters into the earth to form groundwater. Water companies pump the groundwater to a water treatment plant, where it is cleaned and treated, and any waste matter removed. During dry spells, when there isn't enough groundwater, water is taken from reservoirs. The water is then pumped through a network of pipes and pumping stations to our homes.

An infrared sensor detects the user's hands and sends out a signal.

The signal is sent to a solenoid valve (a device that turns an electrical signal into motion). The solenoid starts the water flow.

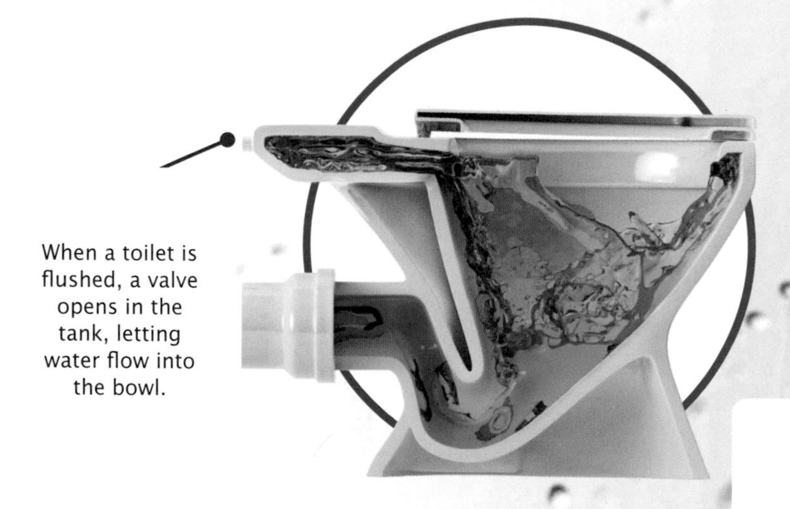

When a toilet is flushed, a valve opens in the tank, letting water flow into the bowl.

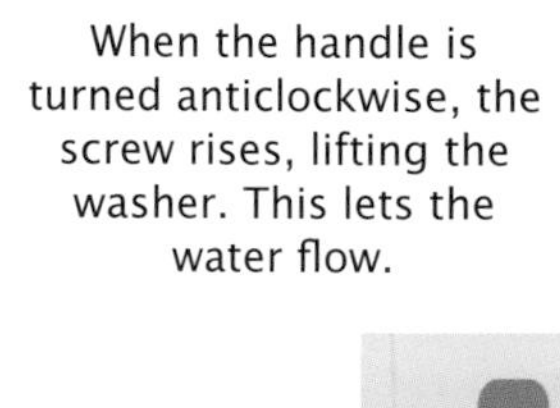

When the handle is turned anticlockwise, the screw rises, lifting the washer. This lets the water flow.

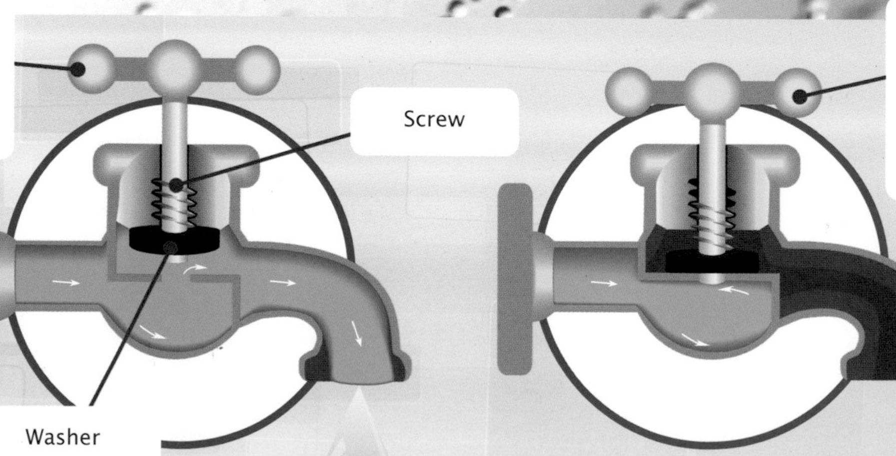
Screw
Washer

When the handle is turned clockwise, the washer is screwed down. This stops the flow of water.

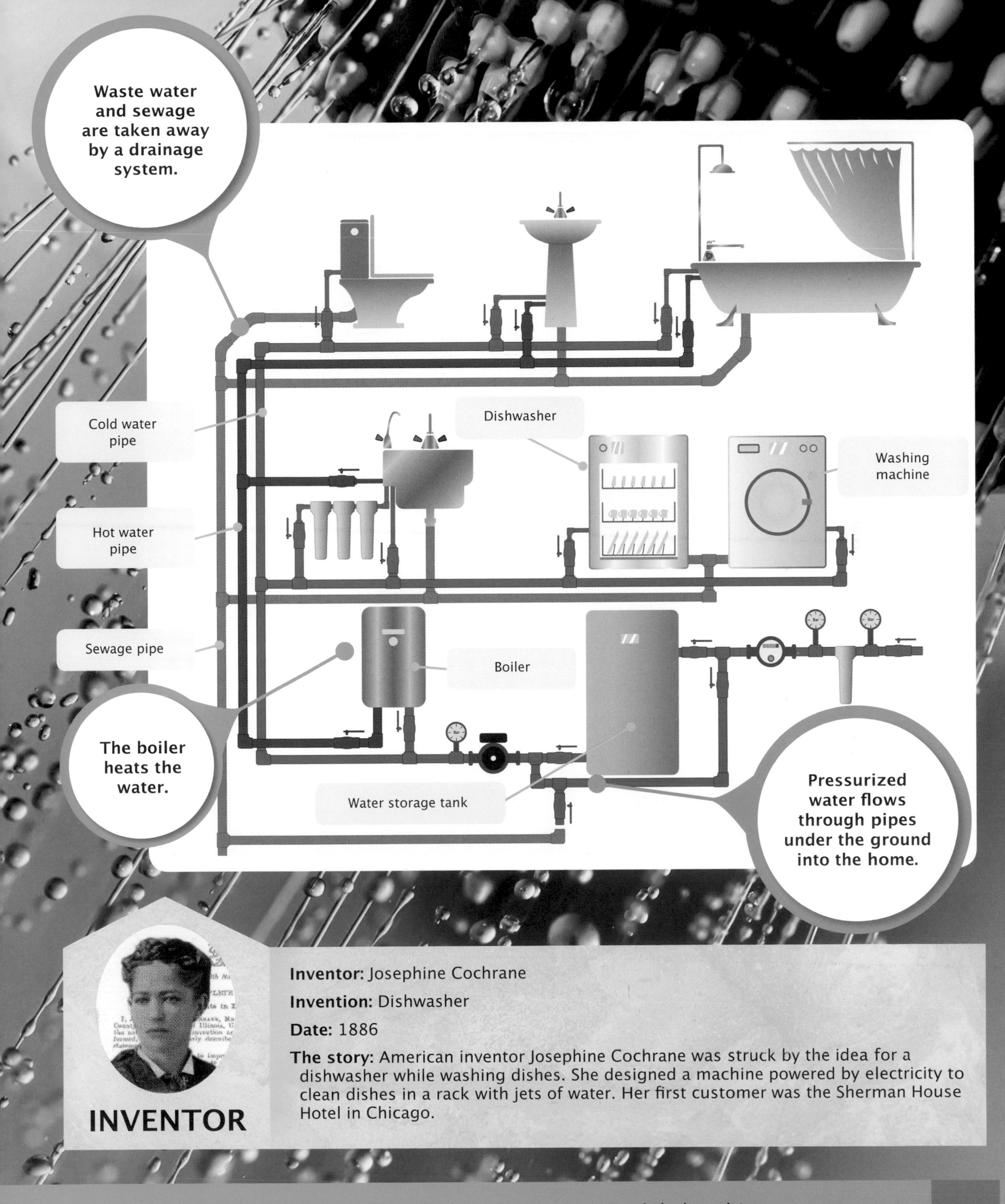
Waste water and sewage are taken away by a drainage system.
Cold water pipe
Hot water pipe
Sewage pipe
Dishwasher
Washing machine
Boiler
Water storage tank
The boiler heats the water.
Pressurized water flows through pipes under the ground into the home.
INVENTOR

Inventor: Josephine Cochrane

Invention: Dishwasher

Date: 1886

The story: American inventor Josephine Cochrane was struck by the idea for a dishwasher while washing dishes. She designed a machine powered by electricity to clean dishes in a rack with jets of water. Her first customer was the Sherman House Hotel in Chicago.

DID YOU KNOW? Keeping the water running while brushing your teeth can waste about 15 litres (30 pints) of water.

Thermos Flasks

Thermos flasks keep cold liquids cold and hot liquids hot by preventing the flow of heat. Heat always flows from a hot place to a cooler place. It can be transferred by conduction, convection, and radiation. A thermos flask prevents all three types of heat transfer.

Glass is a poor conductor of heat, so it reduces the transfer of heat by conduction.

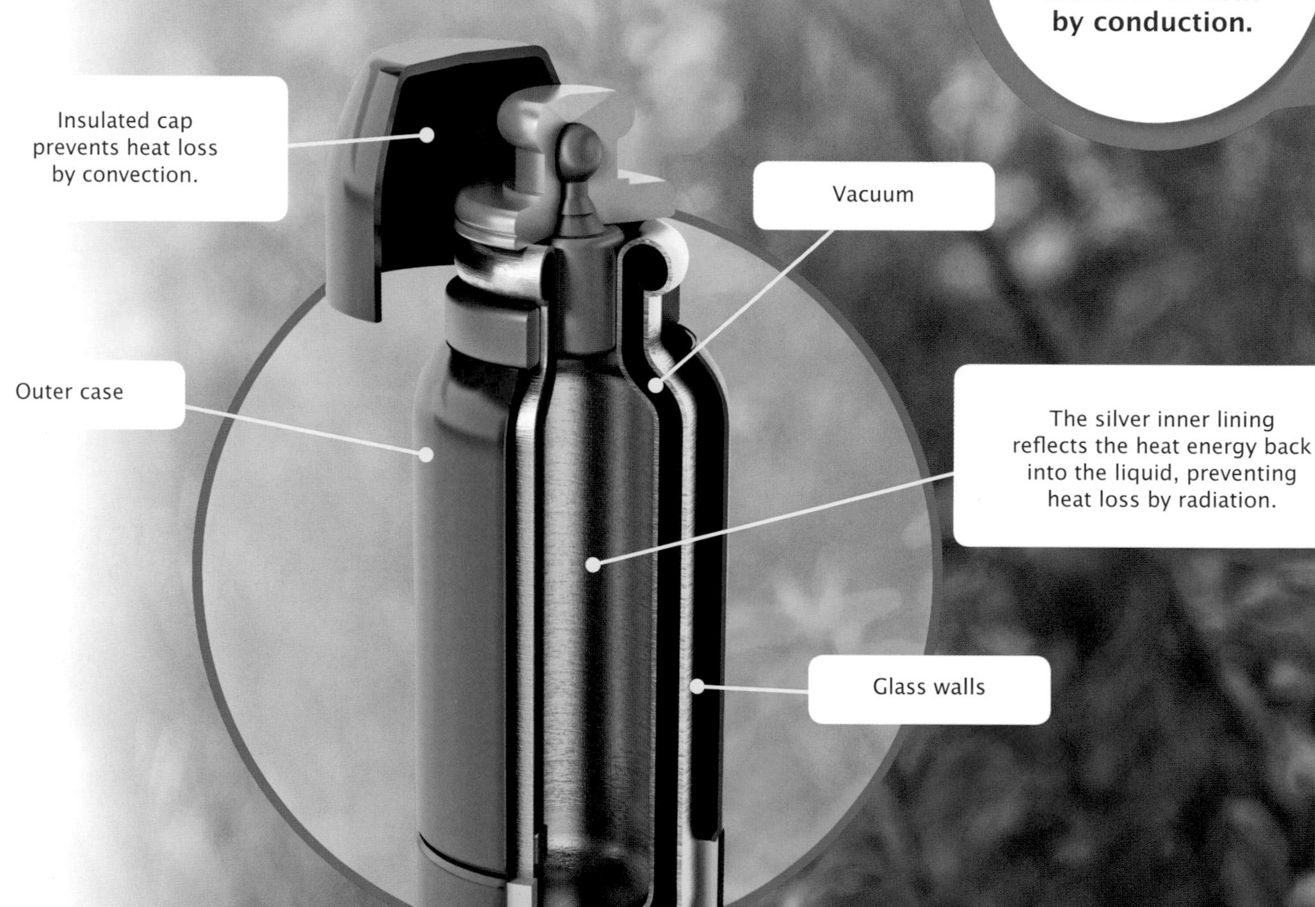

Insulated cap prevents heat loss by convection.
Vacuum
Outer case
The silver inner lining reflects the heat energy back into the liquid, preventing heat loss by radiation.
Glass walls

INVENTOR

Inventor: James Dewar

Invention: Thermos flask

Date: 1892

The story: Scottish chemist and physicist Sir James Dewar invented the Dewar flask, which later became known as the thermos flask, to study how gas can be changed into a liquid. His aim was to keep the liquefied gas as cold as possible.

The air is removed from between the two glass walls, creating a vacuum. This prevents heat transfer through convection and conduction.
Hot or cold liquid
Different forms of heat transfer
Convection is heat transfer due to motion of a liquid or gas.
Heat
Conduction is the transfer of heat through physical contact between objects. Metal is a good conductor of heat. Plastic and glass are not.
Radiation is heat transferred by electromagnetic waves.

DID YOU KNOW? The liquid fuel used in space rockets is kept cold using thermos technology.

Refrigerators

The technology of refrigerators is based on a simple principle: when a gas is compressed, it gets warmer; and when it expands, it cools. A pipe running partly inside and partly outside the refrigerator is filled with gas. Outside the refrigerator the gas is compressed, while inside the refrigerator the pipe widens, so the gas expands and cools to a liquid.

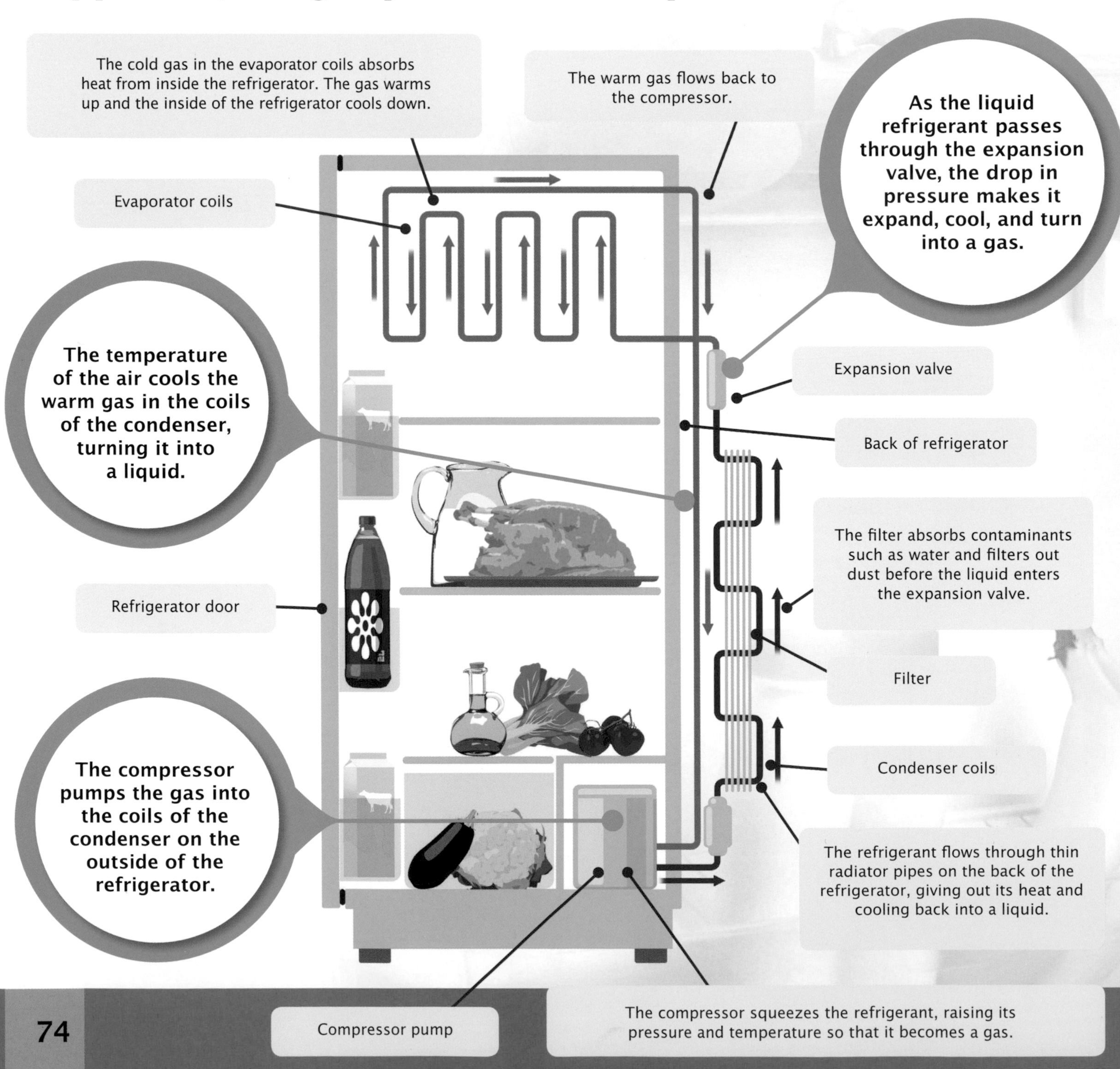

The cold gas in the evaporator coils absorbs heat from inside the refrigerator. The gas warms up and the inside of the refrigerator cools down.
The warm gas flows back to the compressor.
As the liquid refrigerant passes through the expansion valve, the drop in pressure makes it expand, cool, and turn into a gas.
Evaporator coils
The temperature of the air cools the warm gas in the coils of the condenser, turning it into a liquid.
Expansion valve
Back of refrigerator
The filter absorbs contaminants such as water and filters out dust before the liquid enters the expansion valve.
Refrigerator door
Filter
The compressor pumps the gas into the coils of the condenser on the outside of the refrigerator.
Condenser coils
The refrigerant flows through thin radiator pipes on the back of the refrigerator, giving out its heat and cooling back into a liquid.
Compressor pump
The compressor squeezes the refrigerant, raising its pressure and temperature so that it becomes a gas.

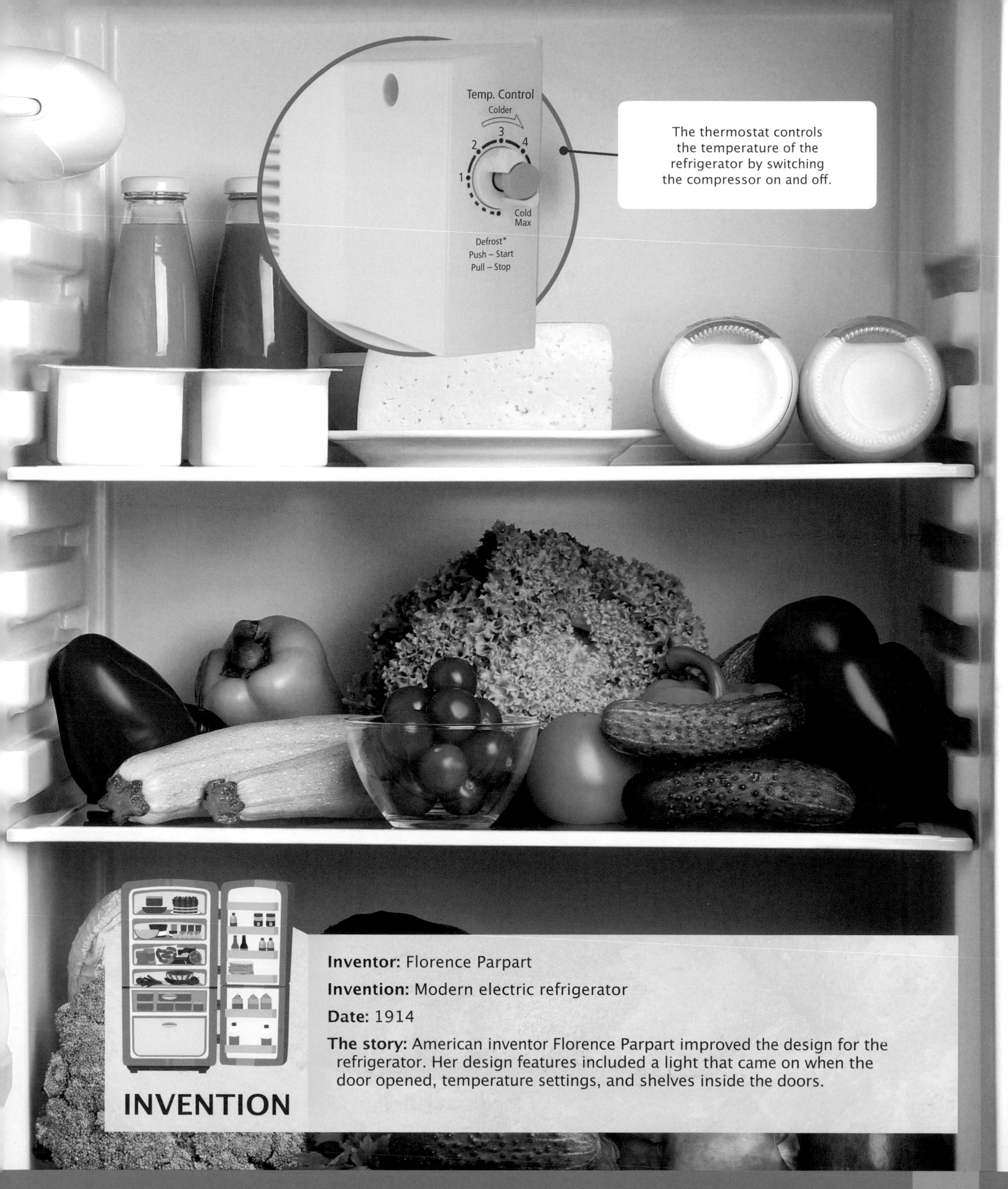
Temp. Control
Colder
1
2
3
4
Cold
Max
Defrost*
Push – Start
Pull – Stop
INVENTION

The thermostat controls the temperature of the refrigerator by switching the compressor on and off.

Inventor: Florence Parpart

Invention: Modern electric refrigerator

Date: 1914

The story: American inventor Florence Parpart improved the design for the refrigerator. Her design features included a light that came on when the door opened, temperature settings, and shelves inside the doors.

DID YOU KNOW? One of the world's largest refrigeration units keeps the Hadron Collider particle accelerator at CERN cool.

Hairdryers

Inside the hairdryer is a heating element, which is a long, thin coil of wire that converts electrical energy into heat energy. A motor drives a fan that draws air in through holes in the side of the hairdryer. The air is warmed as it passes over the heating element before being blown out of the front of the dryer.

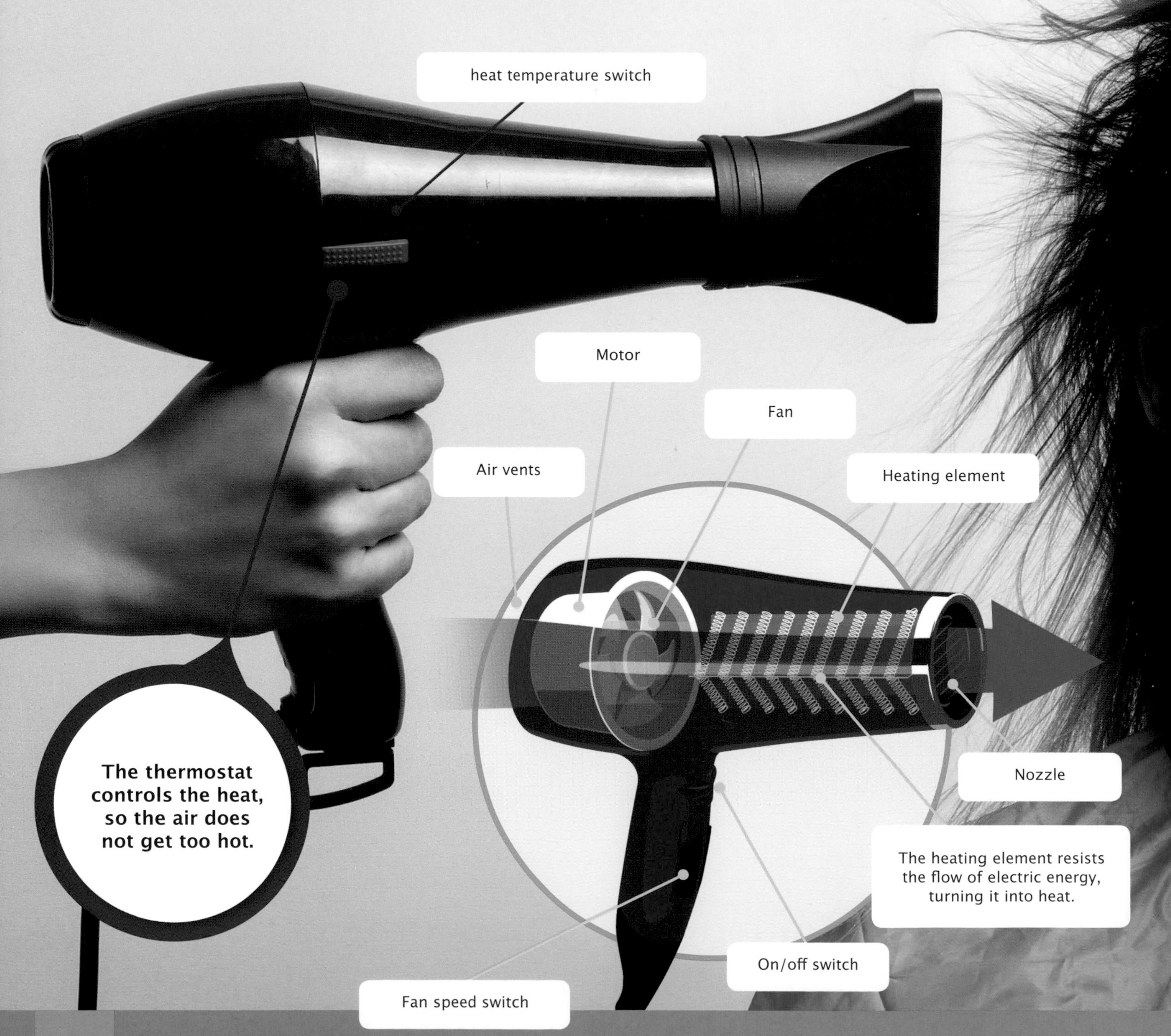
heat temperature switch
Motor
Fan
Air vents
Heating element
Nozzle
The heating element resists the flow of electric energy, turning it into heat.
On/off switch
Fan speed switch
The thermostat controls the heat, so the air does not get too hot.

INVENTOR

Inventor: Alexander Godefroy

Invention: Hairdryer

Date: 1890

The story: French hairdresser Alexander Godefroy invented the first hairdryer. His customers sat on a chair and wore a bonnet that was attached to the chimney pipe of a gas stove. It was not portable.

Quiet hairdryer

Engineers have produced a lighter, quieter design of hairdryer. Its intelligent heating control prevents the air becoming too hot.

Sensors measure exit air temperature 20 times per second and sends data to microprocessor monitoring heating element.

Blades spin at up to 110,000rpm at an inaudible frequency.

The rubber isolation mount stops the electric motor from vibrating against the casing, reducing noise.

DID YOU KNOW? The first handheld hairdryer was produced in 1920. It was made of metal and very heavy.

Lightbulbs

An incandescent lightbulb has a simple structure. At the base are two metal contacts—the ends of an electrical circuit. They are attached to a very thin filament made of tungsten. The filament is housed within a glass bulb filled with an inert (non-reactive) gas, such as argon.

Tungsten is used as a filament because it has an extremely high melting point.

How incandescent bulbs work

When the incandescent lightbulb is attached to a power supply, an electric current flows from one contact to the other, passing through the wires and filament. The thin tungsten filament is resistant to the flow of electricity, so it quickly heats up, releasing energy in the form of light. The filament gets extremely hot, but it doesn't burn because there is no air inside the glass bulb, just an inert gas.

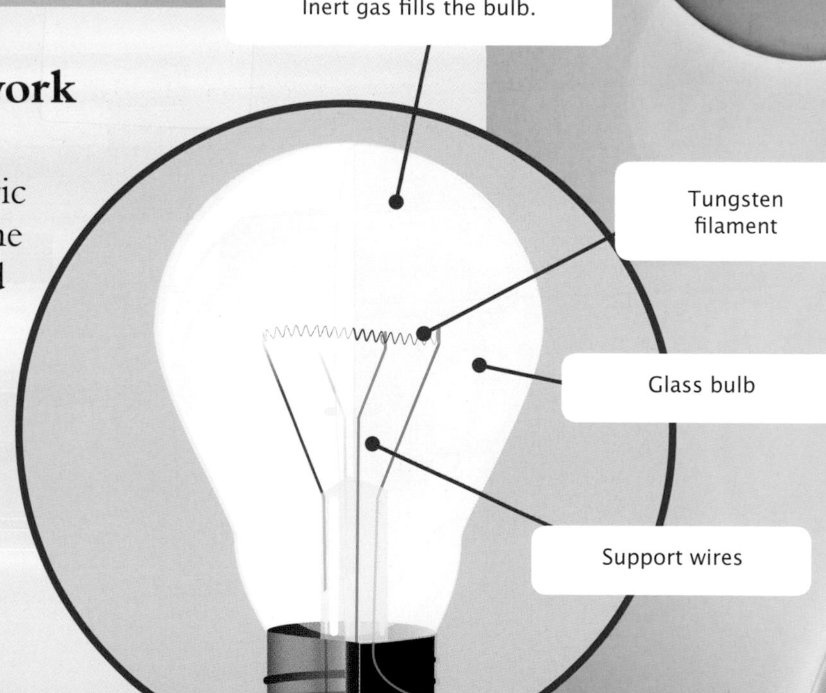
Inert gas fills the bulb.
Tungsten filament
Glass bulb
Support wires
Metal contacts

INVENTOR

Inventor: Nick Holonyak, Jr.

Invention: LED bulb

Date: 1962

The story: American engineer Nick Holonyak, Jr. invented the light-emitting diode (LED). LEDs don't have a filament that will burn out, and don't get very hot. Their illumination is caused by the movement of electrons in a semiconductor material.

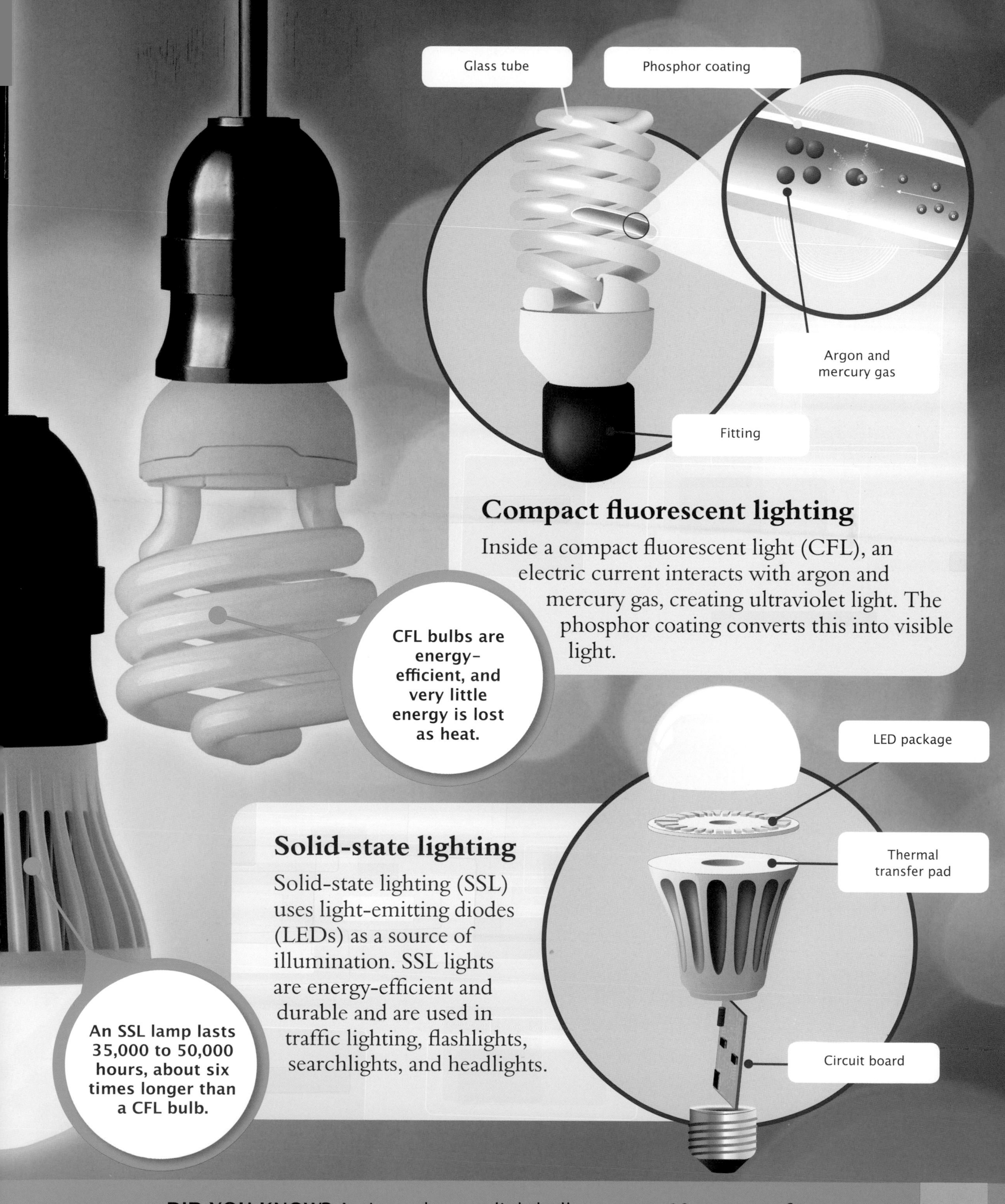
Glass tube
Phosphor coating
Argon and mercury gas
Fitting
CFL bulbs are energy-efficient, and very little energy is lost as heat.
LED package
Thermal transfer pad
Circuit board
An SSL lamp lasts 35,000 to 50,000 hours, about six times longer than a CFL bulb.

Compact fluorescent lighting

Inside a compact fluorescent light (CFL), an electric current interacts with argon and mercury gas, creating ultraviolet light. The phosphor coating converts this into visible light.

Solid-state lighting

Solid-state lighting (SSL) uses light-emitting diodes (LEDs) as a source of illumination. SSL lights are energy-efficient and durable and are used in traffic lighting, flashlights, searchlights, and headlights.

DID YOU KNOW? An incandescent lightbulb converts 10 percent of its energy into light—and an LED nearly 100 percent of its energy into light.

Microwave Ovens

Microwave ovens cook food using high-powered electromagnetic waves, known as microwaves. A device called a magnetron converts electricity from the mains outlet into microwaves, which it sends into the oven through a tube called a waveguide. The microwaves penetrate the food, making the molecules inside it vibrate and causing the food to heat up.

Microwaves bounce off the reflective walls of the cooking compartment and into the food.

Microwaves have wavelengths greater than those of visible light.

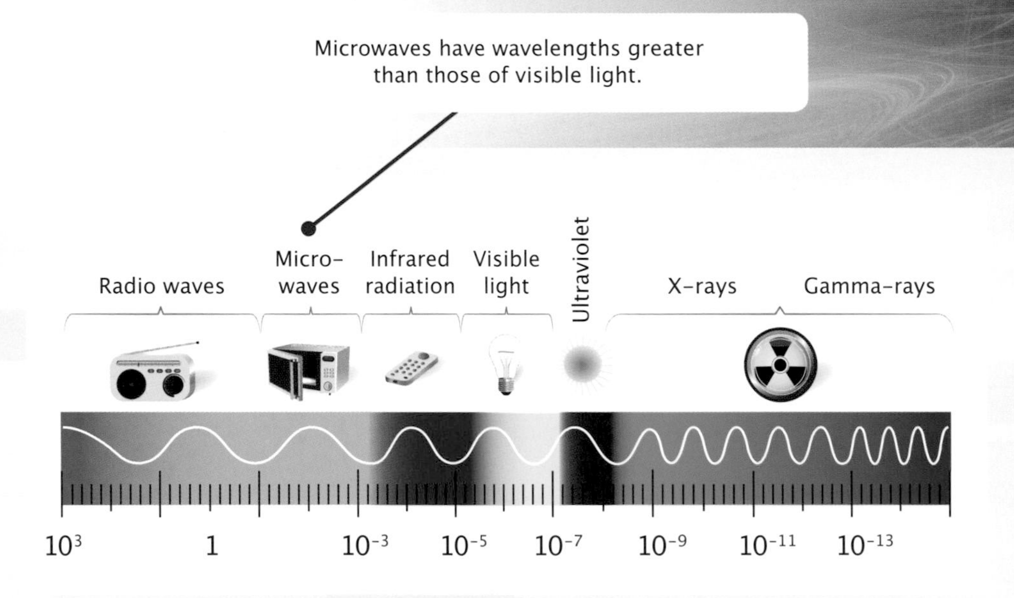

Radio waves
Micro-waves
Infrared radiation
Visible light
Ultraviolet
X-rays
Gamma-rays
10^{3}
1
10^{-3}
10^{-5}
10^{-7}
10^{-9}
10^{-11}
10^{-13}

Electromagnetic spectrum

The electromagnetic spectrum is made up of different types of energy, all with their own wavelength. Microwaves are about 12 cm (4.7 in). They are very high energy, but can harm living tissue, which is why microwave ovens have thick metal walls.

The door contains a metal mesh. The small holes in the mesh stop microwaves from escaping while letting visible light out, so we can see into the cooking compartment.

DID YOU KNOW? It is possible to transmit data using microwaves. They are used by NASA for deep space communication.

INVENTION

Inventor: Percy Spencer

Invention: Microwave oven

Date: 1947

The story: American engineer Percy Spencer was experimenting with microwaves when a magnetron melted his chocolate. He tried placing popcorn kernels near the magnetron, and they popped. This discovery led him to design the microwave oven.

The waveguide directs the microwaves into the cooking compartment.

Cooling fan

The magnetron contains two spinning ring magnets that heat electrons from the electricity and generate the microwaves.

The capacitor boosts the power supply to the magnetron.

Microwaves heat the moisture inside the popcorn kernels, making them pop.

The turntable rotates so the food cooks evenly.

The transformer reduces the voltage of the electricity from the mains supply so the microwave can operate.

Ovens

Gas ovens generate heat using a gas-fuelled burner. When the oven's temperature dial is raised, it opens a valve, letting gas flow to the pilot flame (a small, continuously burning flame). The flame gets bigger, igniting the burner. When the oven has reached the selected temperature, a thermostat will shut off the gas supply to the burner, switching it on again only when the temperature starts to drop.

Electric ovens

Electric ovens contain top and bottom heating elements. Electrical power heats the elements, which heat the cooking compartment. When the right temperature is reached, the thermostat sends a signal to the circuit board, cutting power to the elements. Convection ovens have a fan to blow the hot air around the oven.

Solar ovens cook using the sun's rays. The rays are all reflected to a central place in the oven, so the heat energy from all the rays adds up to make it very hot.

Silver surfaces reflect the heat of the sun into the cooking compartment.

INVENTOR

Inventor: Lloyd Groff Copeman

Invention: Electric oven

Date: 1912

The story: American inventor Lloyd Groff Copeman designed the first electric oven. It was made from a wooden frame housing two metal boxes. His design included a thermostat to control the heating element. It also had an automatic timer.

Induction cooktops

An induction cooktop consists of a ceramic surface with an electromagnetic coil beneath it. When it is switched on, an electric current passes through the coil, creating a magnetic field. This induces several small electric currents in the base of a saucepan or pot placed on the cooktop. The heat comes from the saucepan itself, not the surface. Induction cooking is highly efficient and provides consistent heat and excellent temperature control. However, only stainless steel or iron saucepans can be used.

Electromagnetic coil
Ceramic top
Iron base on pot
The control dials turn on the electricity and control the thermostat.
The pot is heated by a process called magnetic induction.
The food in the cooking compartment is surrounded by hot air. It is heated by convection.

DID YOU KNOW? An oven used in the metal industry is called a furnace. An oven used for making pottery is called a kiln.

Washing Machines

Soap is placed in the detergent tray. It can also be added directly to the inner drum.

Washing machines contain two drums. The inner, rotating drum holds the clothes, and the outer drum holds the water, which flows into and out of the inner drum during the course of the wash. A heating element warms up the water, and a thermostat controls its temperature. An electric pump removes the water from the drum when the wash is over. A pipe sends clean water into the machine, and a second pipe lets out the waste water.

The programmer

An electronic device called a programmer makes the washing maching go through a series of steps to wash and rinse the clothes, then spin them to remove the water.

With a top-loading washing machine, clothes are loaded through a door at the top.

Thor

INVENTION

Inventor: Alva J. Fisher

Invention: Washing machine

Date: 1901

The story: American engineer Alva J. Fisher named the first washing machine Thor. It consisted of a cylinder, which rotated while the clothes were held in position by several spikes. It made eight rotations clockwise, then changed direction. It did not have an on/off switch. Power was cut by pulling the plug out.

DID YOU KNOW? Washing powder for use in a washing machine was invented in 1916.

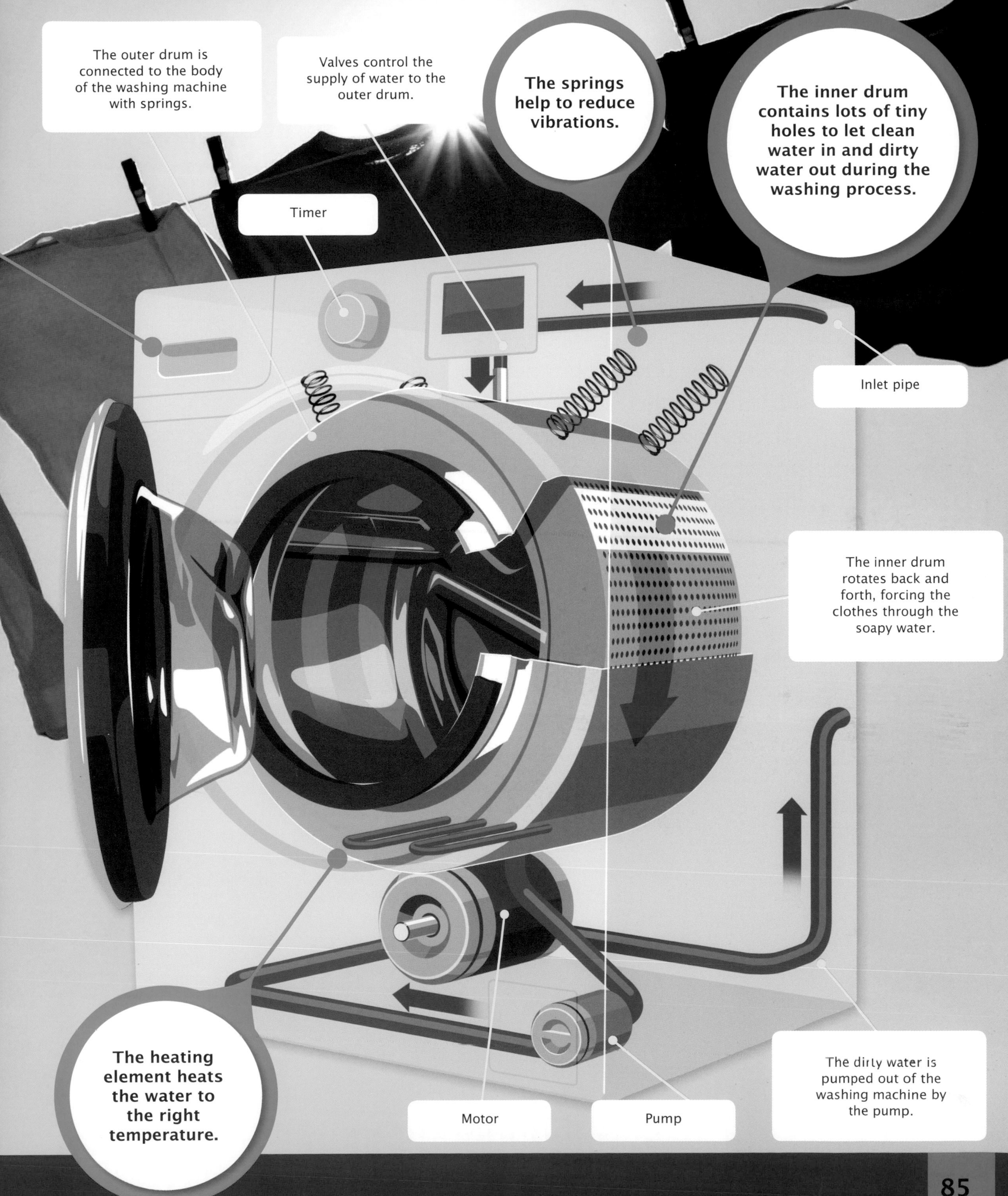
The outer drum is connected to the body of the washing machine with springs.
Valves control the supply of water to the outer drum.
The springs help to reduce vibrations.
The inner drum contains lots of tiny holes to let clean water in and dirty water out during the washing process.
Timer
Inlet pipe
The inner drum rotates back and forth, forcing the clothes through the soapy water.
The heating element heats the water to the right temperature.
Motor
Pump
The dirty water is pumped out of the washing machine by the pump.

Glasses

For someone with good eyesight, light travels to the lens of the eye, which focuses the light onto the retina at the back of the eye. If someone is farsighted, close-up objects look blurred because the lens of the eye focuses light behind the retina. They need glasses with convex lenses, which shorten the path of the light. If someone is shortsighted, distant objects look blurred because the lens of the eye focuses light in front of the retina. They need glasses with concave lenses, which lengthen the path of the light.

Bifocals and varifocals

Some people need glasses for seeing both long distances and close-up. Bifocal lenses split the lens into two parts. Varifocal lenses gradually change from long-distance at the top to short-distance at the bottom.

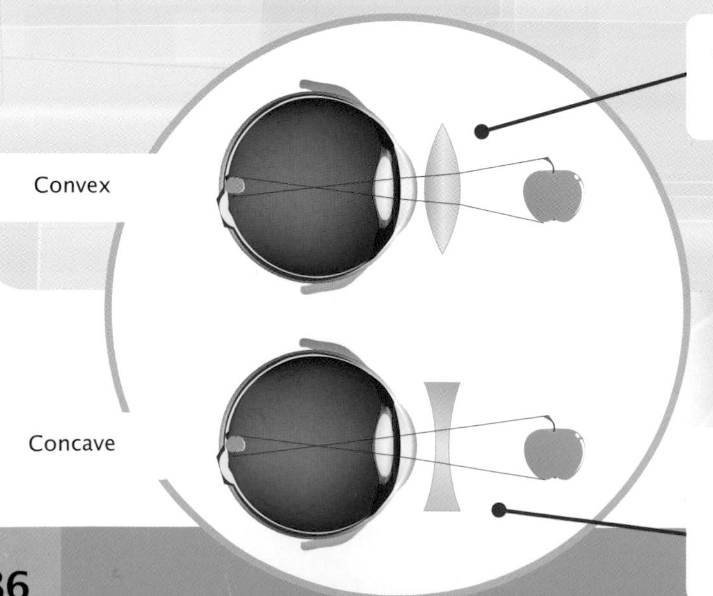
Convex
Concave

A convex lens causes the light rays to meet at a point closer to the lens—on the retina.

A concave lens causes the light rays to travel farther and meet at a focal point farther from the lens—again on the retina.

An optician checks the eye and prescribes the lenses needed to see clearly.

INVENTOR

Inventor: Hermann von Helmholtz

Invention: Ophthalmoscope

Date: 1851

The story: German physicist Hermann von Helmholtz invented the ophthalmoscope. His aim was to discover why the pupil is black in certain conditions but looks red in other conditions.

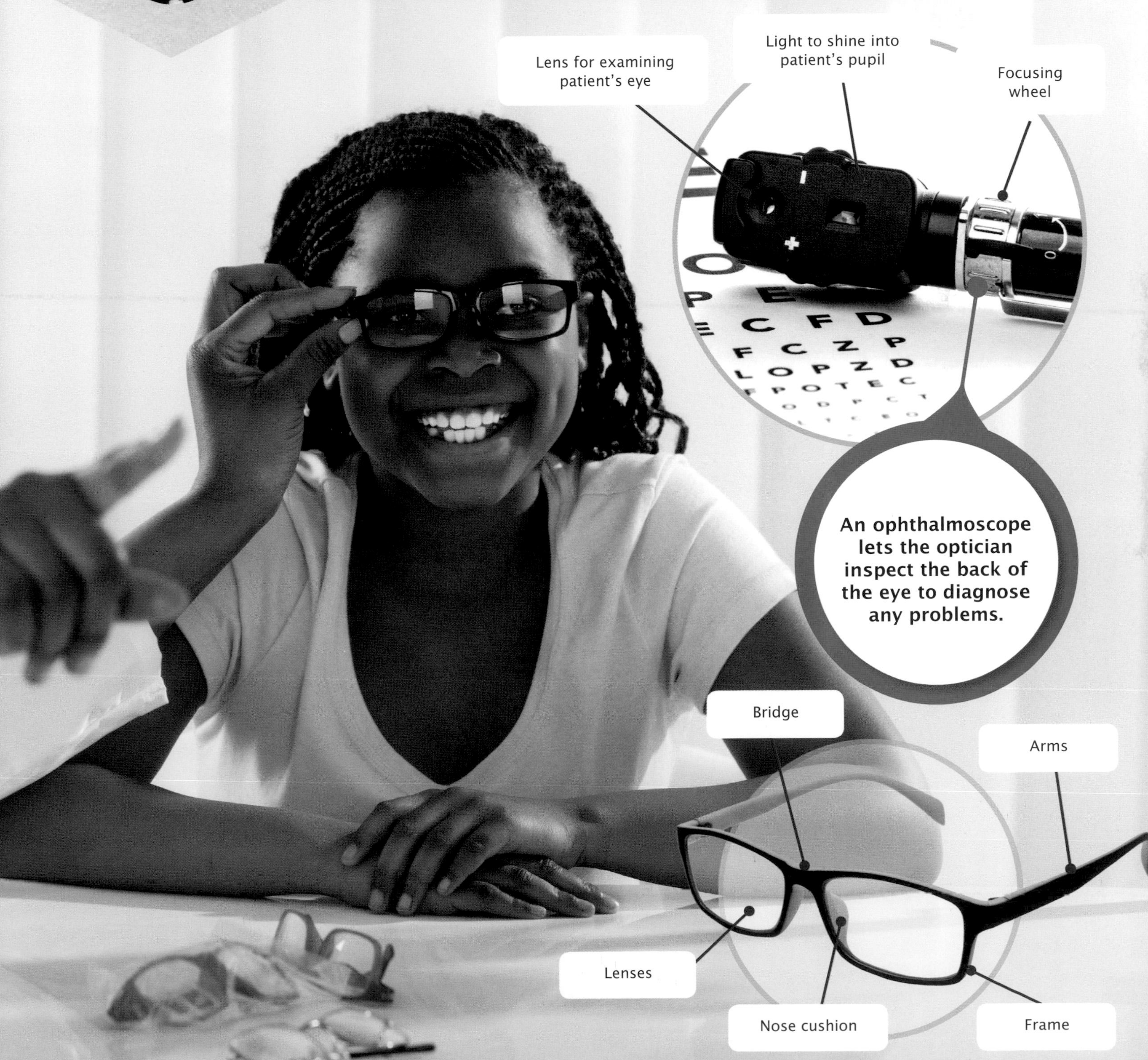
Lens for examining patient's eye
Light to shine into patient's pupil
Focusing wheel
Bridge
Arms
Lenses
Nose cushion
Frame

An ophthalmoscope lets the optician inspect the back of the eye to diagnose any problems.

DID YOU KNOW? Lenses in glasses are not made of glass. They are made from plastic that can be treated with a filter to protect eyes from harmful ultraviolet (UV) rays.

Hearing Aids

The two main kinds of hearing aid are analog and digital. Analog hearing aids convert sound waves into electrical signals, which are then amplified. Digital hearing aids convert sound waves into numerical codes before amplifying them.

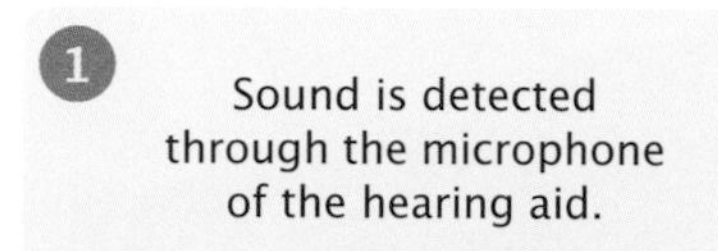
1
Sound is detected through the microphone of the hearing aid.

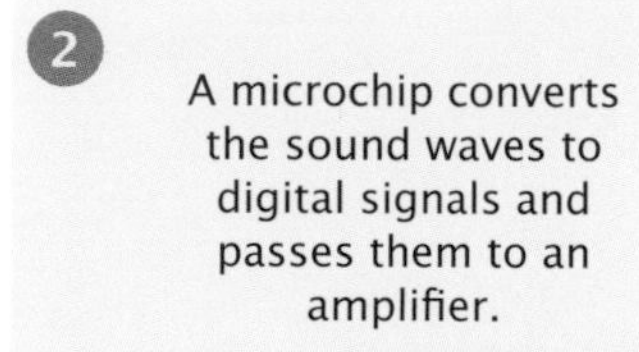
2
A microchip converts the sound waves to digital signals and passes them to an amplifier.

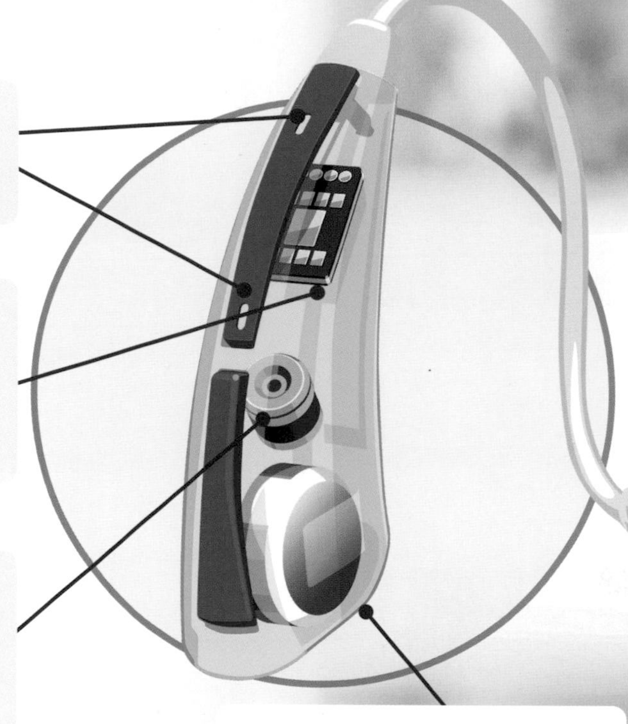
3
The amplifier strengthens the digital signals and passes them to the speaker.
Small, rechargeable batteries power the hearing aid.

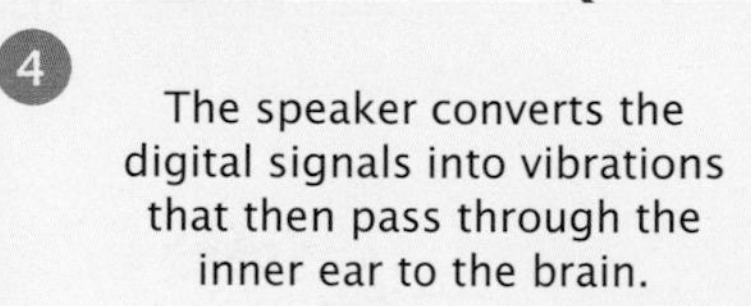
4
The speaker converts the digital signals into vibrations that then pass through the inner ear to the brain.

Telecoil

A telecoil is a small, magnetic coil inside the hearing aid. It helps the user hear conversations on a telephone. It also enables the user to connect to induction loops.

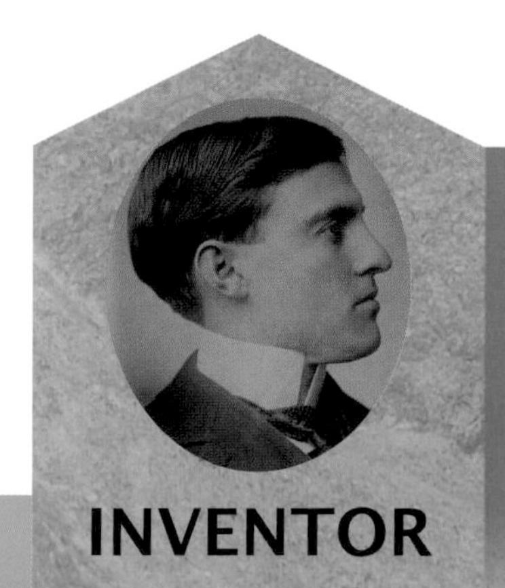

INVENTOR

Inventor: Miller Reese Hutchison

Invention: First electronic hearing aid

Date: 1902

The story: Miller Reese Hutchison designed the first portable hearing aid, called Acousticon. It worked by using a carbon microphone from a telephone to amplify sound.

The earbud is inserted into the ear canal.
Digital hearing aids can be programmed to amplify some sounds more than others.
Some hearing aids are waterproof, so they can be worn while showering or swimming.
T

Induction loop

An induction loop is a sound system found in public places such as schools, cinemas, concert halls, and airports. A loop of wire placed around a room produces an electromagnetic signal that can be received by hearing aids used by people who are partially deaf. A person speaks into a microphone. The sound is strengthened by an amplifier and sent to an antenna that relays the signal directly to the hearing aid. This eliminates background noise.

DID YOU KNOW? Hearing is dependent on tiny hairs deep inside the ear.

X-ray Machines

An X-ray machine is similar to a camera, but it photographs the inside of the body. Inside an X-ray machine is a tube that contains a filament. An electric current passes through the filament to heat it, knocking electrons off the filament surface. They fly through the tube, creating high-energy X-ray photons. The X-rays are directed into a narrow beam that is passed through the patient onto a photographic plate to create an image of the patient's bones.

CAT scanner

X-rays show just one view of the body. A computed axial tomography (CAT) scanner is a machine that creates an image of a slice through the body. It rotates around the body taking a series of X-rays, which are compiled by a computer to show the depth and position of its internal structures.

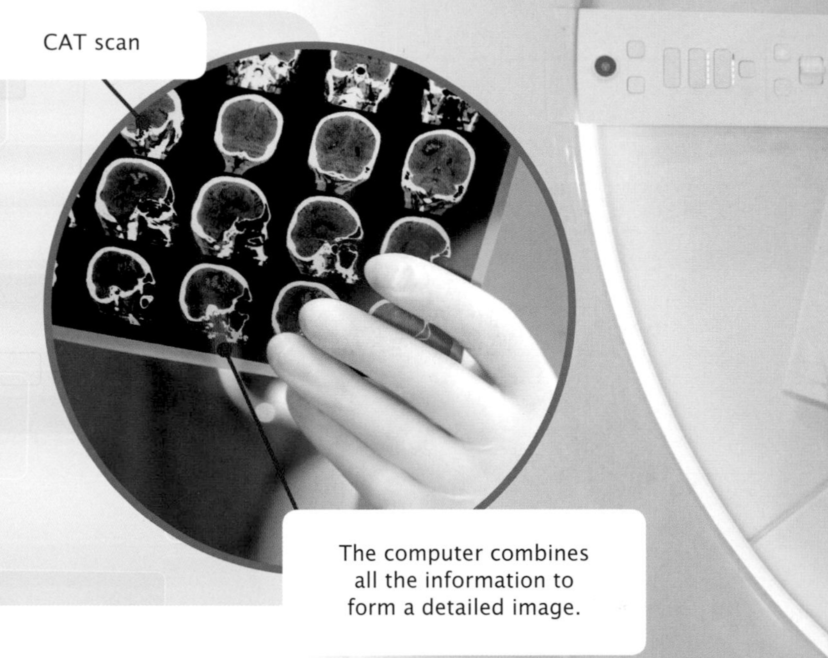
CAT scan
The computer combines all the information to form a detailed image.

The white areas are the bones, which absorb the X-rays, so they do not pass through them.

The X-ray clearly shows where the bone is broken.

The black areas are the soft tissue, which don't show up because the X-rays pass through them.

The patient lies on the table, which slides into the ring-shaped scanner. The table moves in stages farther into the scanner so it can scan the next section or "slice."

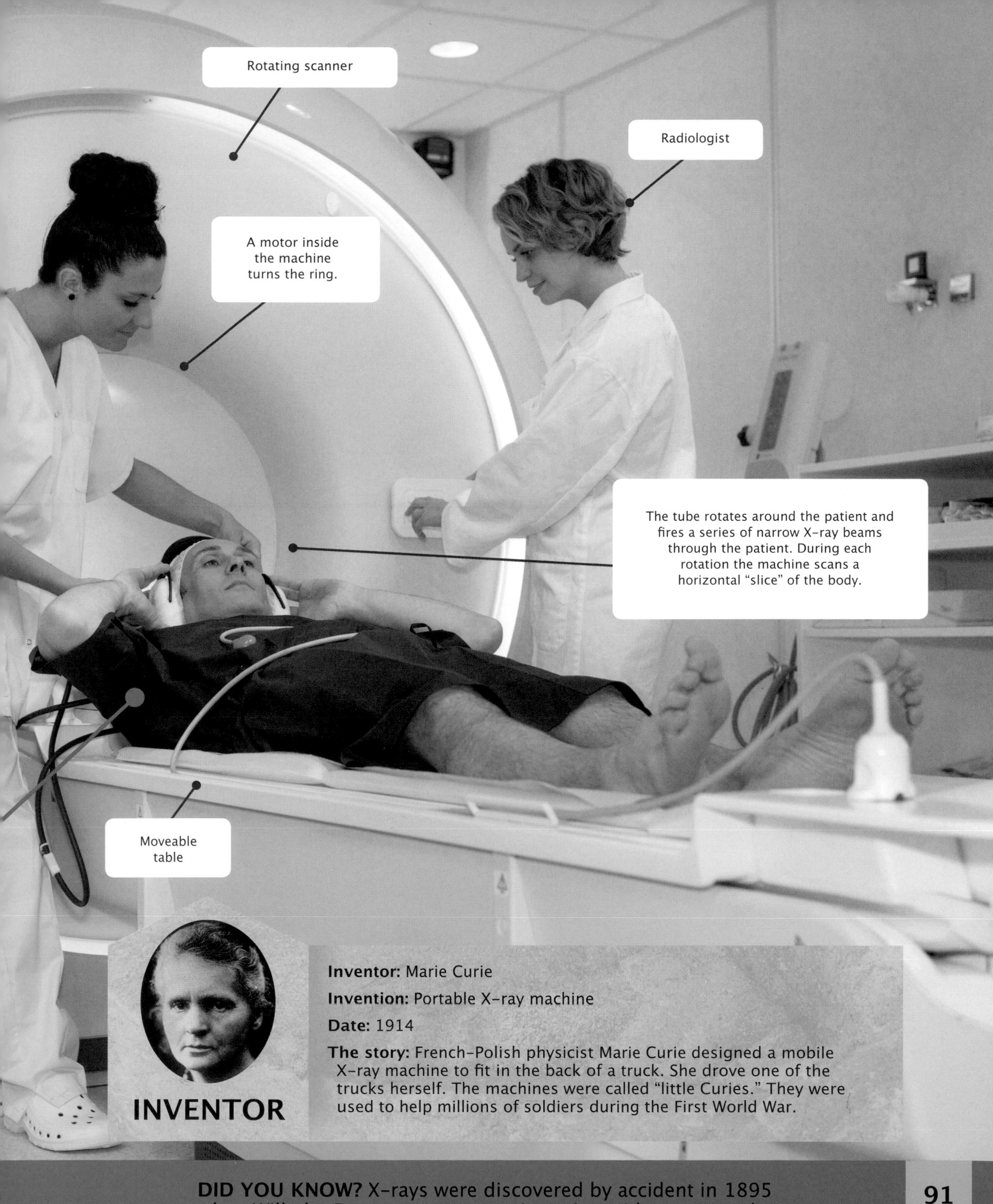
Rotating scanner
Radiologist
A motor inside the machine turns the ring.
The tube rotates around the patient and fires a series of narrow X-ray beams through the patient. During each rotation the machine scans a horizontal "slice" of the body.
Moveable table

INVENTOR

Inventor: Marie Curie

Invention: Portable X-ray machine

Date: 1914

The story: French-Polish physicist Marie Curie designed a mobile X-ray machine to fit in the back of a truck. She drove one of the trucks herself. The machines were called "little Curies." They were used to help millions of soldiers during the First World War.

DID YOU KNOW? X-rays were discovered by accident in 1895 when Wilhelm Roentgen was experimenting with vacuum tubes.

Pacemakers

A pacemaker is surgically implanted under the skin in the chest or abdomen of patients who need help to maintain their heart's regular rhythm. Electrodes (sensors that pick up electrical signals) detect the heart's rhythm and send data through wires to a microchip. If the rhythm is abnormal, the microchip directs a battery-powered generator to send electrical pulses through the wires to the heart.

Microchip

The pacemaker's microchip can "learn" the patient's pattern of heart activity and adjust to mimic it. It can monitor blood temperature and breathing rate, and adjust its output if the patient changes activity, such as when exercising.

Leadless pacemaker

This is a small device that can be placed directly into a patient's heart through a vein in the leg. There are no wires, and it has a battery that lasts approximately 12 years. It works in the same way as a traditional pacemaker by sensing changes in the patient's body related to activity levels, and adjusting the heart rate accordingly.

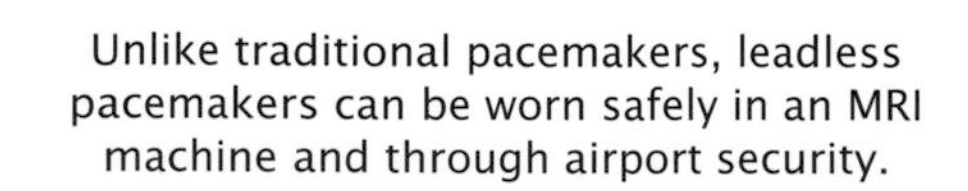

Unlike traditional pacemakers, leadless pacemakers can be worn safely in an MRI machine and through airport security.

INVENTOR

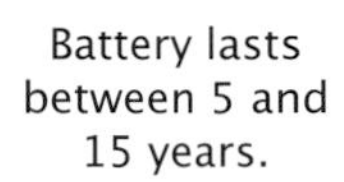

Inventor: Wilson Greatbatch

Invention: Pacemaker

Date: 1958

The story: American engineer Wilson Greatbatch invented the first successful pacemaker when he was trying to record the sound of a heartbeat. He used the wrong transistor, producing a pulse with the same rhythm as a heart.

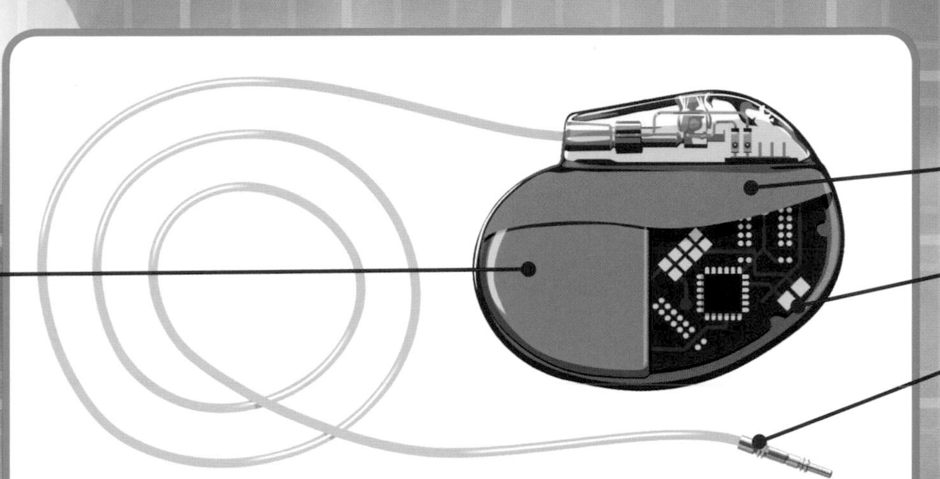

Battery lasts between 5 and 15 years.
Case
Receiver
Electrodes
Pacemaker
The electrodes stimulate the upper and lower chambers of the heart to make it contract in a regular rhythm.
The pacemaker is sealed in a waterproof case, so no body fluids can leak in.

DID YOU KNOW? Each year, about one million people worldwide have a pacemaker implanted.

Prosthetic Limbs

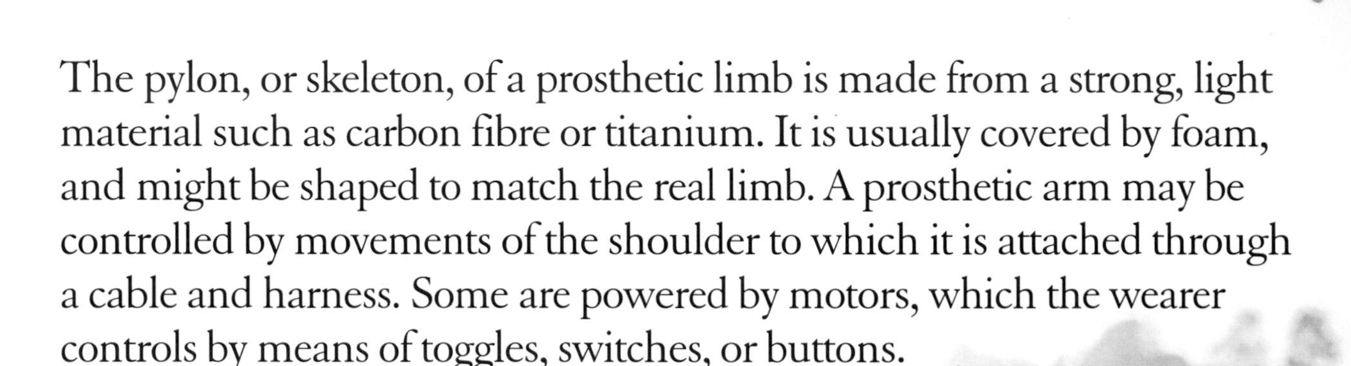

The pylon, or skeleton, of a prosthetic limb is made from a strong, light material such as carbon fibre or titanium. It is usually covered by foam, and might be shaped to match the real limb. A prosthetic arm may be controlled by movements of the shoulder to which it is attached through a cable and harness. Some are powered by motors, which the wearer controls by means of toggles, switches, or buttons.

Myoelectric prosthetics

Myoelectric prosthetics are controlled by electric signals generated in the muscles. When the muscles contract, electrodes placed on the surface of the skin measure the muscle movement and move the limb.

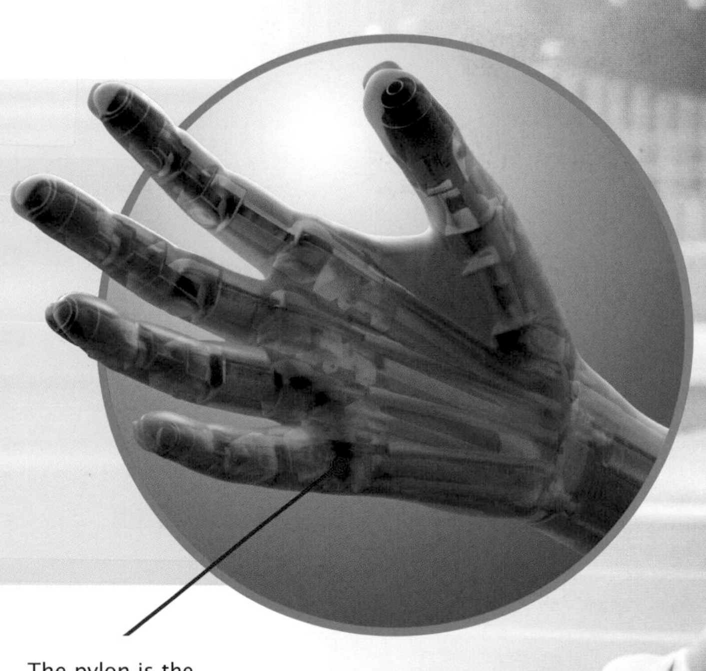

The pylon is the internal skeleton of the prosthetic limb.

DESIGNER

Designer: Sophie de Oliveira Barata

Product: Prosthetic limbs

Date: 2018

The story: Sculptor and special-effects designer Sophie de Oliveira Barata has been described as "the undisputed queen of personalized prosthetics." She designs and makes fun alternative limbs, as well as realistic limbs where she matches skin tone, hair, freckles, nails, and limb shape exactly.

A prosthetic sock achieves a more secure fit.
The prosthetic feet, called cheetahs, store energy when they are compressed, and spring back into shape when the pressure is released.
Soft lining is added to the inside of the socket to prevent damage to the skin and underlying tissues.
Attachment
Curved cheetahs
A flexible silicone skin is stretched to make it translucent, and applied over the foam to make it look more lifelike.
Rubber grip
The socket slots into the patient's residual limb.

Neural interfacing

Some prosthetic limbs are directly controlled by the brain using "neural interfacing." Tiny electrodes are placed in the brain to measure neural activity. The patient thinks about what kind of movement they want to make. This generates motor signals in the brain, which are decoded by a computer. The computer then directs the prosthetic device to perform the required movement.

DID YOU KNOW? A prosthetic tail was made for Winter the dolphin, who lost her tail as a baby in a crab trap.

Medical Technology

Medical technology monitors and diagnoses a person's health. Doctors use stethoscopes to listen to a patient's heart and thermometers to record a patient's temperature. Blood pressure cuffs are used to check blood pressure. Two measurements are taken—the systolic pressure, when the heart contracts, and the diastolic pressure, when the heart muscle relaxes.

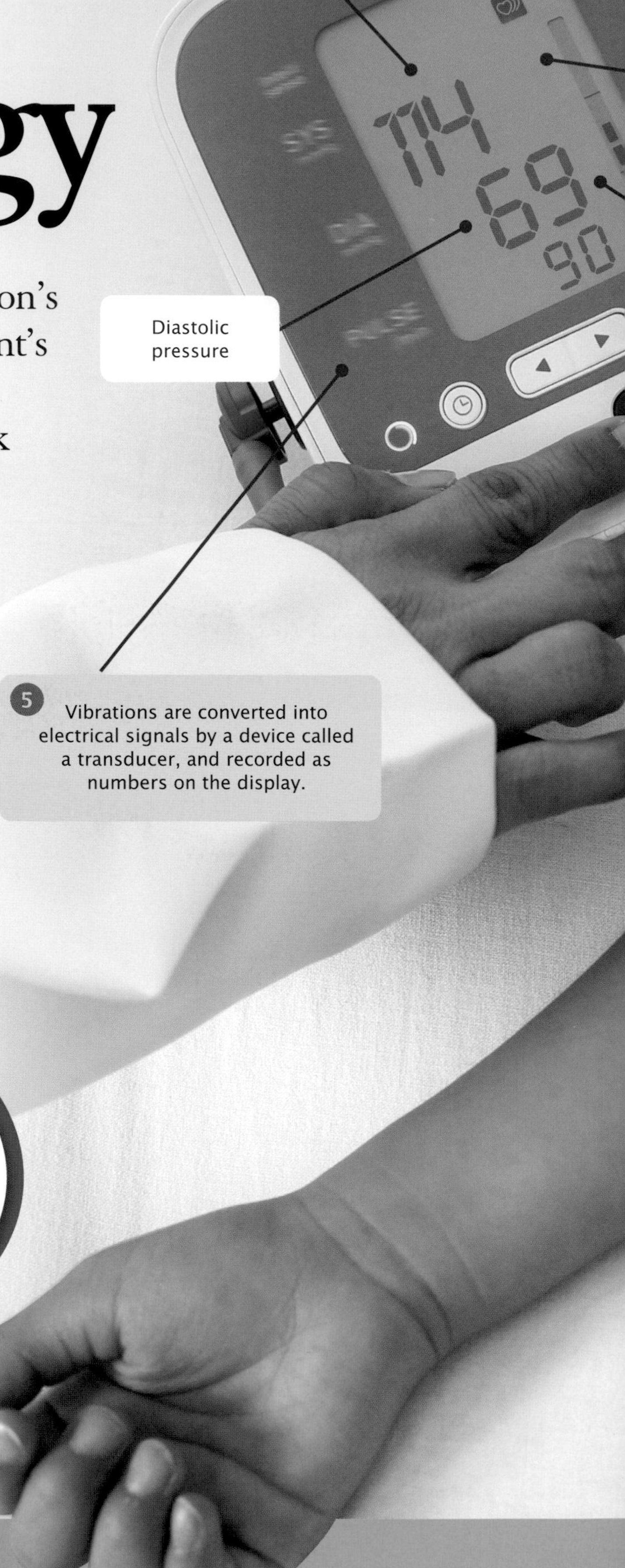

Systolic pressure
Diastolic pressure
5 Vibrations are converted into electrical signals by a device called a transducer, and recorded as numbers on the display.

Glucometer

A glucometer tests the amount of glucose (sugar) in the blood. A sensor inside a patch takes blood readings through the skin. The sensor collects one reading per minute and sends the data wirelessly to a remote monitor. It triggers an alarm if levels are not within the normal range.

82
87
99

Glucose levels are digitally displayed and stored on a portable monitor.

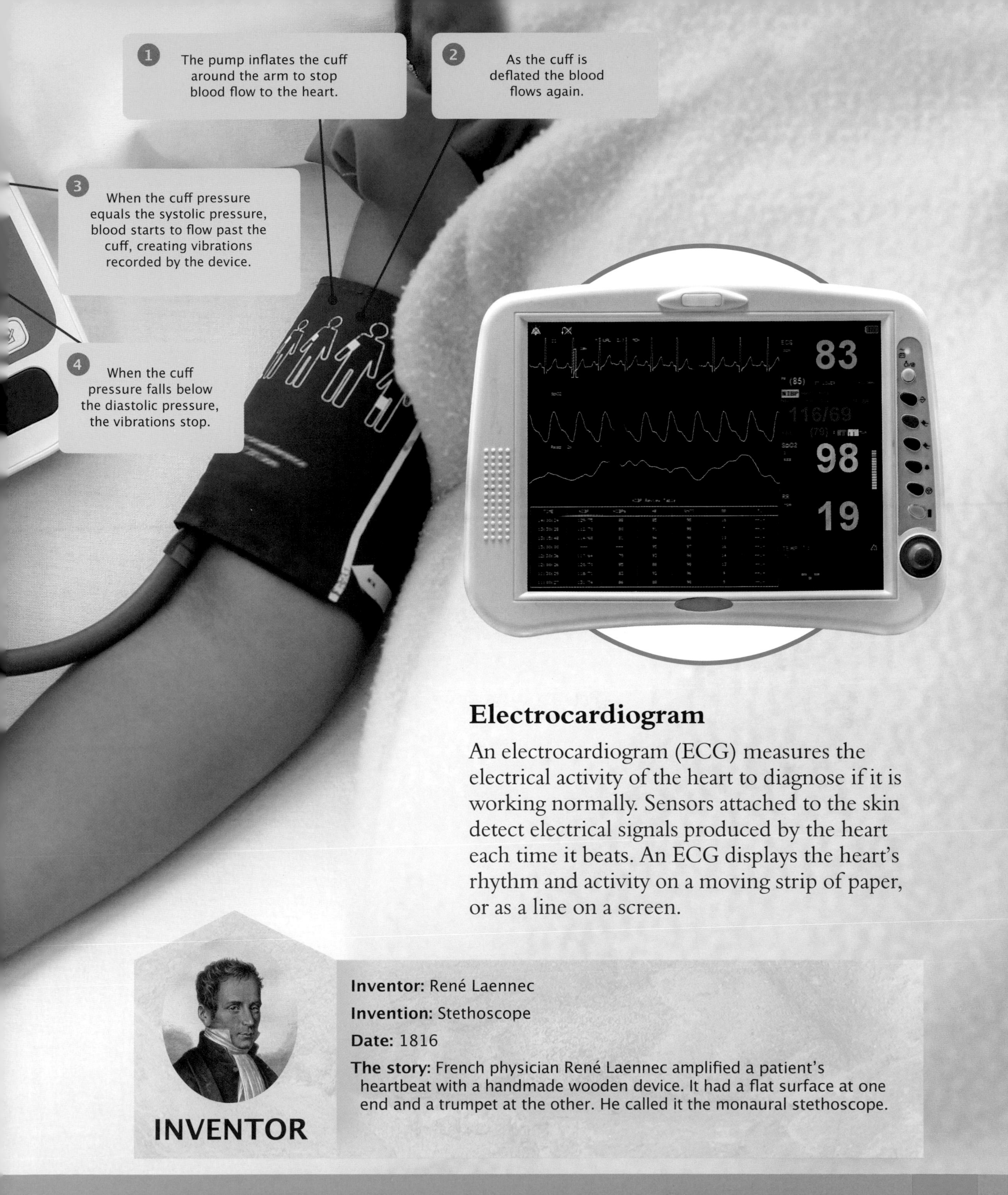
1 The pump inflates the cuff around the arm to stop blood flow to the heart.
2 As the cuff is deflated the blood flows again.
3 When the cuff pressure equals the systolic pressure, blood starts to flow past the cuff, creating vibrations recorded by the device.
4 When the cuff pressure falls below the diastolic pressure, the vibrations stop.
83
116/69
98
19

Electrocardiogram

An electrocardiogram (ECG) measures the electrical activity of the heart to diagnose if it is working normally. Sensors attached to the skin detect electrical signals produced by the heart each time it beats. An ECG displays the heart's rhythm and activity on a moving strip of paper, or as a line on a screen.

INVENTOR

Inventor: René Laennec

Invention: Stethoscope

Date: 1816

The story: French physician René Laennec amplified a patient's heartbeat with a handmade wooden device. It had a flat surface at one end and a trumpet at the other. He called it the monaural stethoscope.

DID YOU KNOW? In 2011 a stethoscope was invented that enables doctors on Earth to hear the heartbeats of astronauts in space.

MRI

A magnetic resonance imaging (MRI) scanner uses powerful tube-shaped magnets to create a magnetic field. Protons inside the body's hydrogen atoms are sensitive to magnetic fields. When a patient lies under the scanner magnets, the protons in their body line up in the same direction.

The magnetic field runs along the length of the scanner.

Radio waves

The MRI sends out short bursts of radio waves to knock the protons out of alignment. When the radio waves are turned off, the protons in different types of tissue realign at different speeds and produce distinct signals. The data is collated by the computer to produce a detailed image of the inside of the body. The process only takes a few seconds.

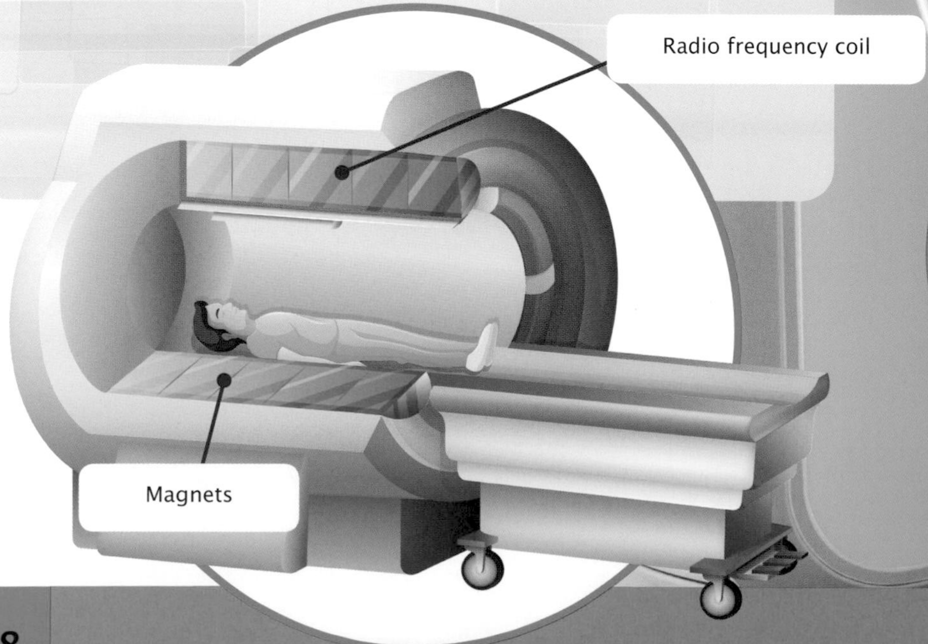

Radio frequency coil

Magnets

Receivers in the scanner detect the radio signals produced by the body's protons returning to their normal spin.

INVENTOR

Inventor: Raymond Damadian

Invention: MRI scanner

Date: 1977

The story: American physician Raymond Damadian created an MRI scanner called "Indomitable" to diagnose cancer. He was the first person to carry out a full body scan. The scan took five hours to produce.

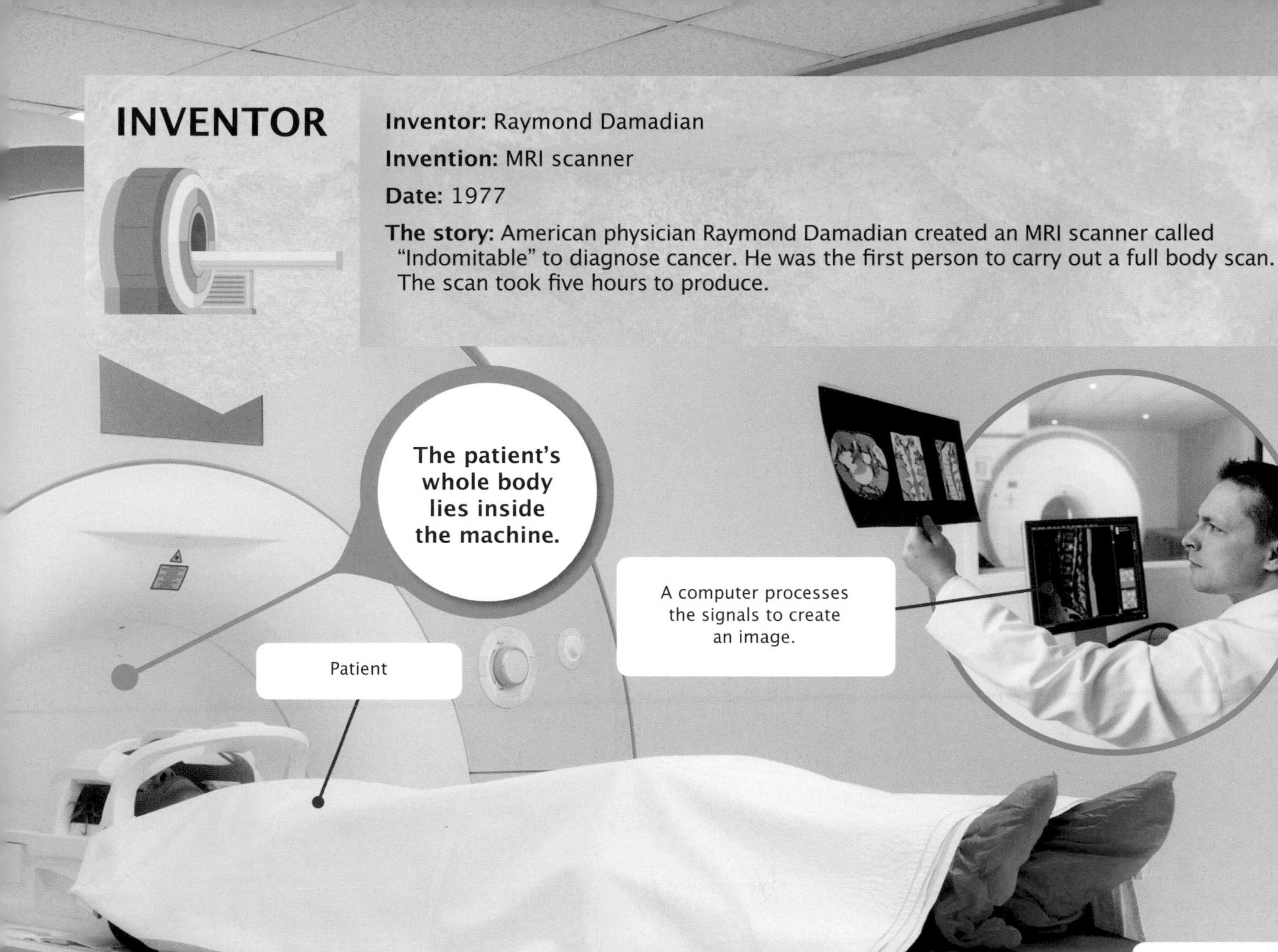

The patient's whole body lies inside the machine.
A computer processes the signals to create an image.
Patient
Table

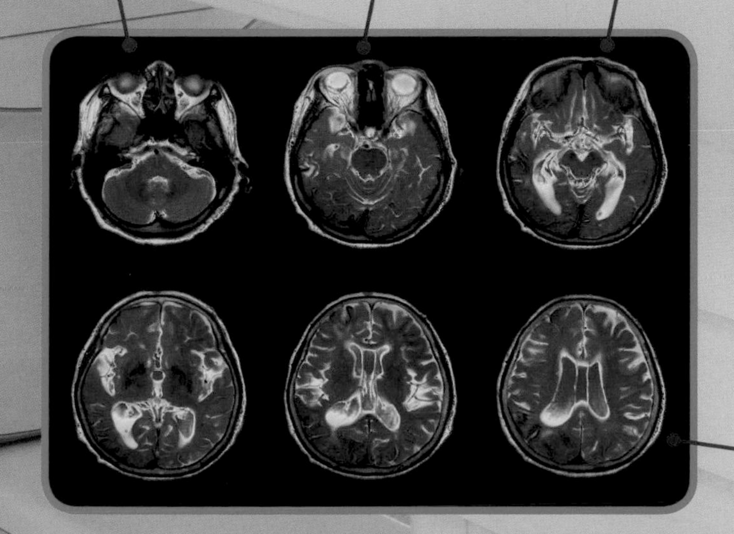

Top of the brain
Middle of the brain
Bottom of the brain

An MRI scan produces images of the body at different depths and angles.

MRI scans

Unlike X-rays, MRI scans show images of soft body tissues such as muscles, brain tissue, lungs, and liver. They can also detect fractures in the skeleton that are too small for X-rays to pick up.

DID YOU KNOW? The most powerful MRI scanners can create a magnetic field 140,000 times stronger than Earth's magnetic field.

Nanotechnology

Nanotechnology is the process of altering atoms and molecules to create new and improved substances and processes. Nanoparticles are measured in nanometres (nm), or one billionth of a metre. This is a million times smaller than an ant. Scientists have developed the scanning tunneling microscope and the atomic force microscope, enabling them to see individual atoms and change them.

Sunscreens

Nanoparticles are used in sunscreen to make it more effective at reflecting ultraviolet light while letting visible light through. As the nanoparticles are smaller than the particles in traditional sunscreens and they are transparent, there is no white residue to rub in and they start working immediately.

Nanotechnology can reconstruct brain cells and restore cognitive function.

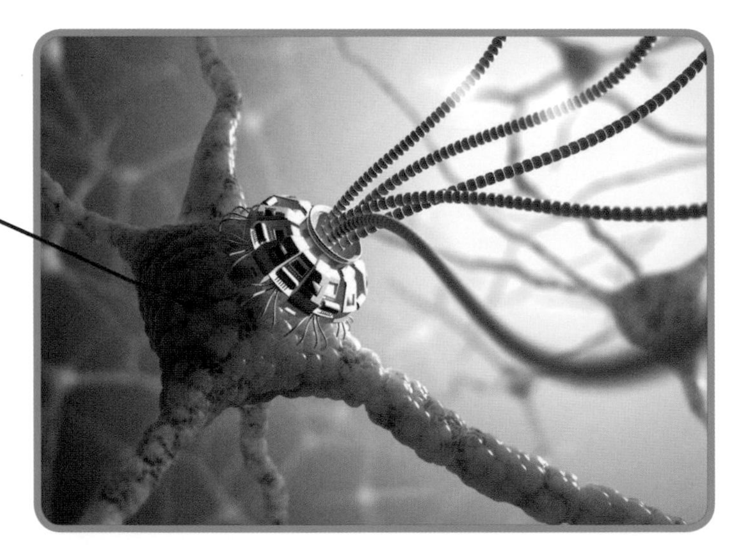

In the future, nanotechnology could be used to make new connections between cells.

Nanotherapeutic drugs can target blood clots and dissolve them away.

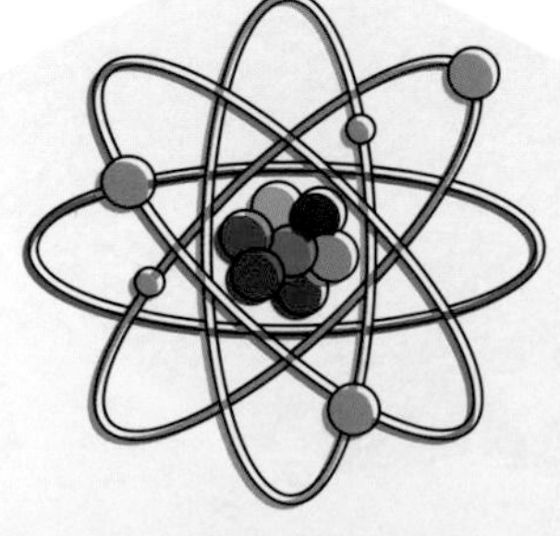

PIONEER

Pioneer: Dr. Richard Feynman

Idea: Nanotechnology

Date: 1959

The story: American physicist Dr. Richard Feynman gave a lecture called "There's Plenty of Room at the Bottom," which theorized about the possibility of manipulating individual atoms and molecules decades before the technology was available to do so.

DID YOU KNOW? Scientists have designed a fluorescent nanoparticle that glows inside the body, making it easier to identify cancer cells and organ damage.

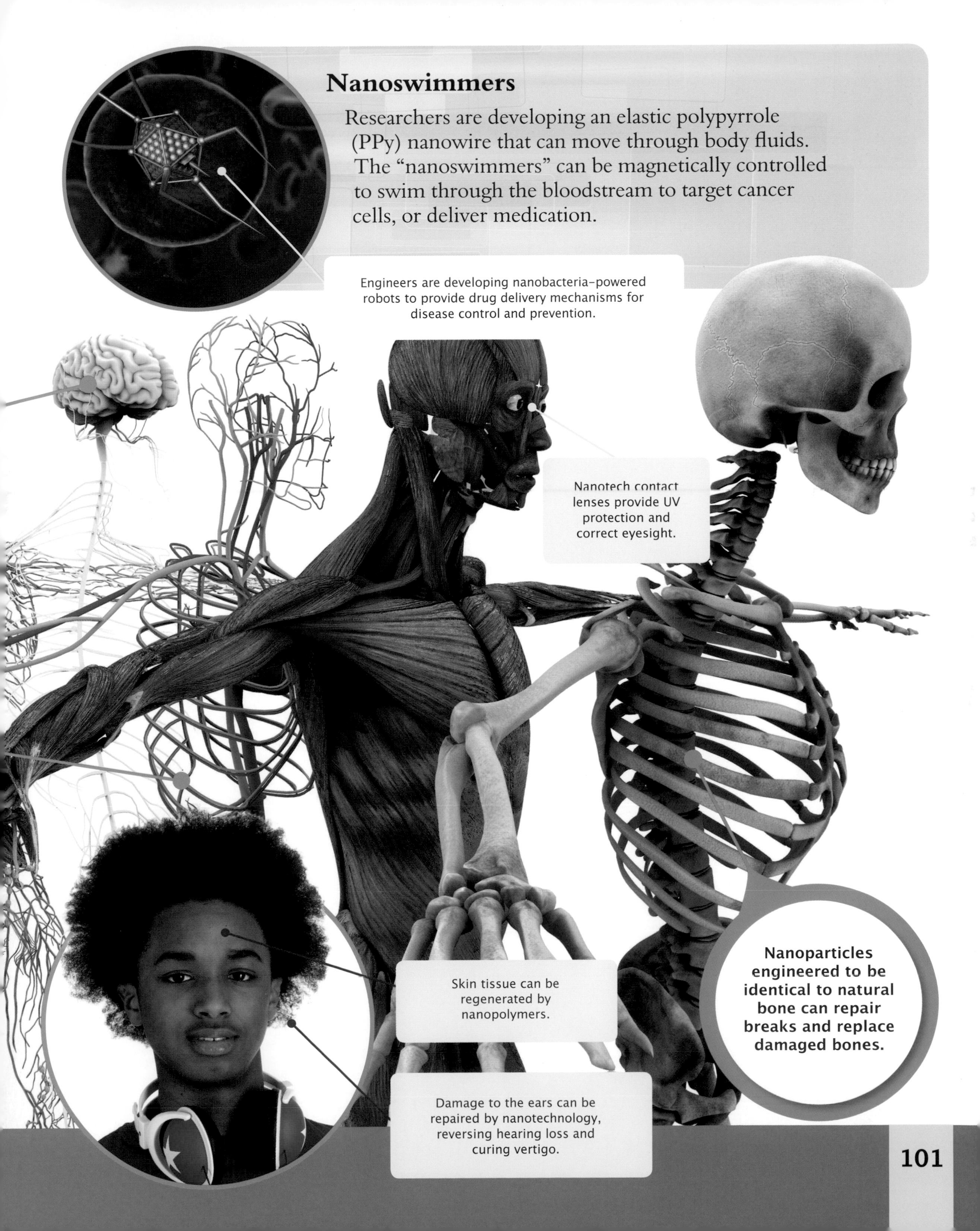
Nanoswimmers
Researchers are developing an elastic polypyrrole (PPy) nanowire that can move through body fluids. The "nanoswimmers" can be magnetically controlled to swim through the bloodstream to target cancer cells, or deliver medication.
Engineers are developing nanobacteria-powered robots to provide drug delivery mechanisms for disease control and prevention.
Nanotech contact lenses provide UV protection and correct eyesight.
Skin tissue can be regenerated by nanopolymers.
Nanoparticles engineered to be identical to natural bone can repair breaks and replace damaged bones.
Damage to the ears can be repaired by nanotechnology, reversing hearing loss and curing vertigo.

RFID Tags

Radio Frequency Identification (RFID) tags are devices that store and update data about a person, animal, or object. They transmit this to an RFID reader using radio waves. RFID tags can be attached to products being bought and sold. They can be embedded within credit cards, travel passes, and smartphones, and are also often implanted in pets and sometimes people.

What do they contain?

RFID tags that are implanted in pets are about the size of a grain of rice. They are enclosed in a non-toxic "bioglass" capsule. Inside the capsule is a microchip that holds an ID number and other data, a capacitor, and a copper coil antenna to send and receive radio signals.

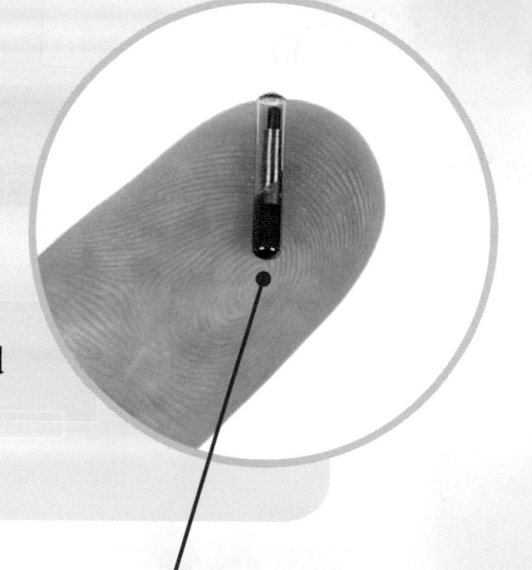

Some pet RFID tags have a special sheath that encourages animal tissue to form around the capsule to hold it in place.

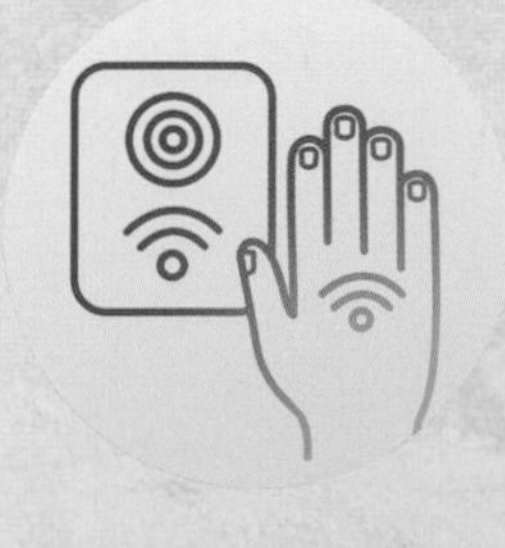

INVENTION

Inventor: Charles Walton

Invention: RFID tag

Date: 1973

The story: American designer Charles Walton designed a portable radio frequency transmitter that stored an identification number to unlock a door without a key. It sent a signal to the reader located by the door. This technology is the basis of the RFID tag.

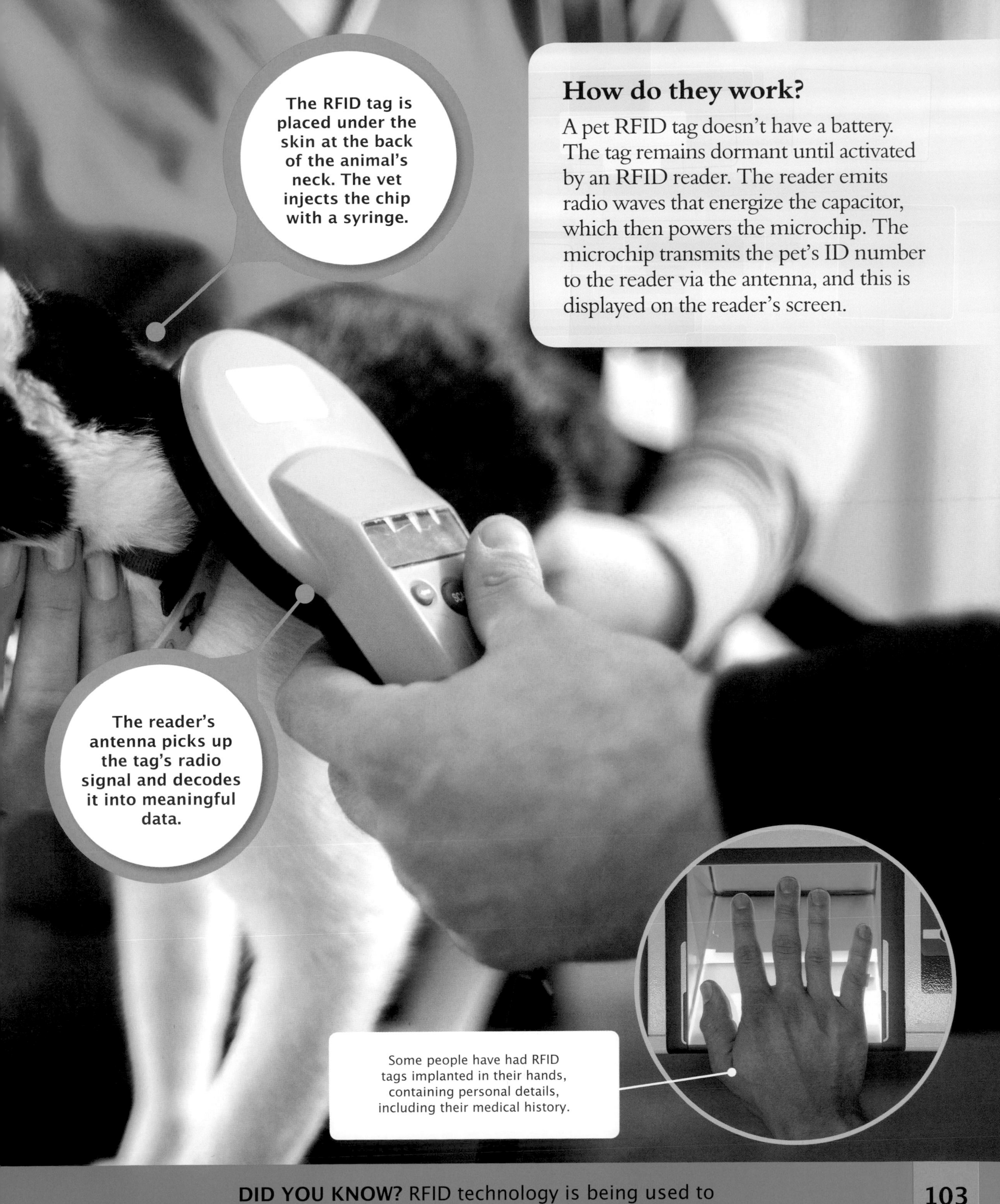
The RFID tag is placed under the skin at the back of the animal's neck. The vet injects the chip with a syringe.
The reader's antenna picks up the tag's radio signal and decodes it into meaningful data.
Some people have had RFID tags implanted in their hands, containing personal details, including their medical history.

How do they work?

A pet RFID tag doesn't have a battery. The tag remains dormant until activated by an RFID reader. The reader emits radio waves that energize the capacitor, which then powers the microchip. The microchip transmits the pet's ID number to the reader via the antenna, and this is displayed on the reader's screen.

DID YOU KNOW? RFID technology is being used to monitor and help protect many endangered animals.

CRISPR Technology

Fruit and vegetables can be genetically altered so they are more resistant to drought and insects.

Many bacteria possess an immune system that enables them to detect and destroy the DNA of a virus that is attacking them. A new technology, known as CRISPR, exploits this ability of bacteria in order to make changes to DNA and possibly cure genetic diseases. CRISPR enables cells to record viruses they have been exposed to and pass protection on through DNA over many generations.

Cas9

Part of the CRISPR system is a protein called Cas9, which is able to seek out, cut, and degrade viral DNA. Scientists have harnessed Cas9's ability as a means of deleting or inserting pieces of DNA in the DNA helix with absolute precision.

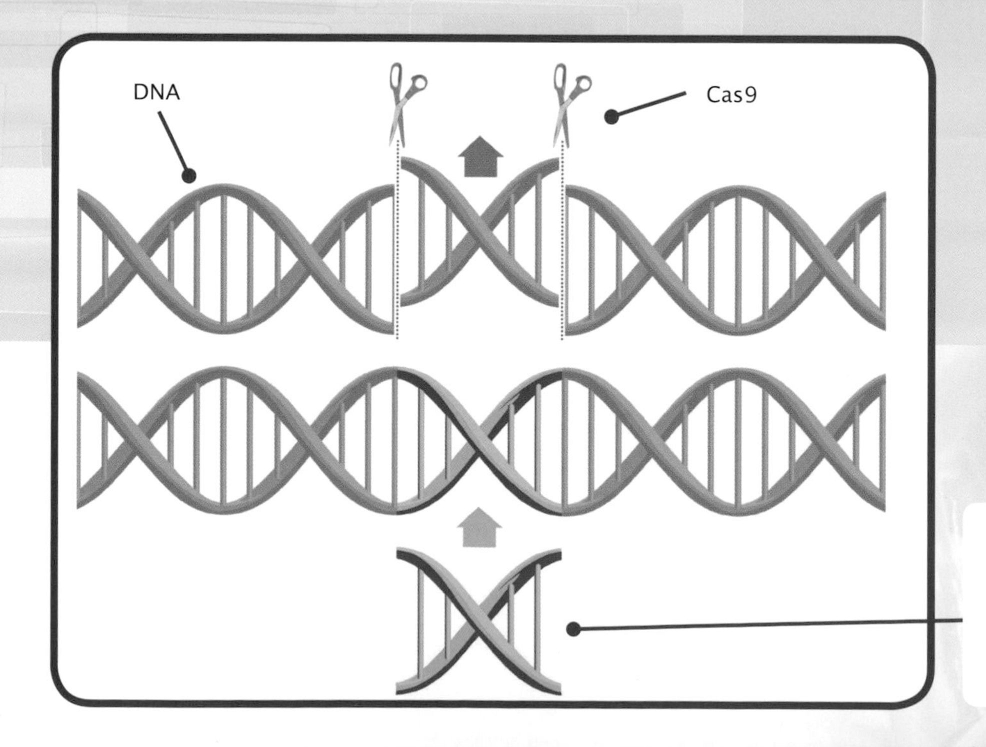

DNA
Cas9

Cas9
DNA

Cells have the ability to detect broken DNA and repair it. The Cas9 protein triggers cells to repair the breaks by integrating new genetic information.

DID YOU KNOW? By targeting cancerous cells in mice using CRISPR technology, scientists have stopped and reduced the cancer growth.

In genetically engineered food, the genes from the DNA of one species of fruit or vegetable are extracted and injected into the genes of an unrelated plant using CRISPR technology.
Maize, soy, squash, and sugar beet are some of the most common genetically modified foods.

INVENTOR

Inventor: Emmanuelle Charpentier (pictured) and Jennifer Doudna

Invention: CRISPR

Date: 2012

The story: American biochemist Jennifer Doudna and French microbiologist and geneticist Emmanuelle Charpentier discovered CRISPR-Cas9 while doing a basic research project aimed at finding out how bacteria fights viral infection.

3D Printing

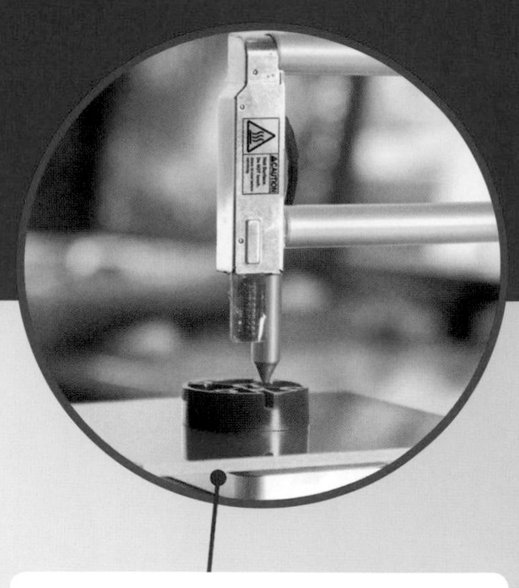

A three-dimensional (3D) printer produces solid objects from a design created on a computer. First, the computer slices the 3D design into thousands of 2D layers. Then it prints it from the bottom up, one layer at a time. Instead of ink, the printer extrudes a material such as molten plastic or powder through a tiny nozzle that moves around as directed by the computer.

3D printers can produce a huge range of products: crockery, toys, even (one day soon) artificial body parts for transplant.

Processes

There are different types of 3D printing. Stereolithography uses liquid resin and a laser to build objects. Ultraviolet light from the laser solidifies the resin and joins it to the layer below. Binder 3D printing uses two separate materials—a fine powder and a liquid glue—to form each layer. The first pass lays down the powder, and the second uses nozzles to apply the binder.

In the future, we may be able to order burgers and other meals from a 3D printer.

INVENTION

Inventor: Chuck Hull

Invention: Stereolithography

Date: 1983

The story: American inventor Chuck Hull is the inventor of the 3D printing process known as stereolithography. This was the world's first commercially successful, rapid 3D printing technology.

Mass production

Products such as sports shoes can be mass produced using a 3D printing process called Digital Light Synthesis. It uses a combination of liquid resin, light, and oxygen to print smooth, durable products very quickly.

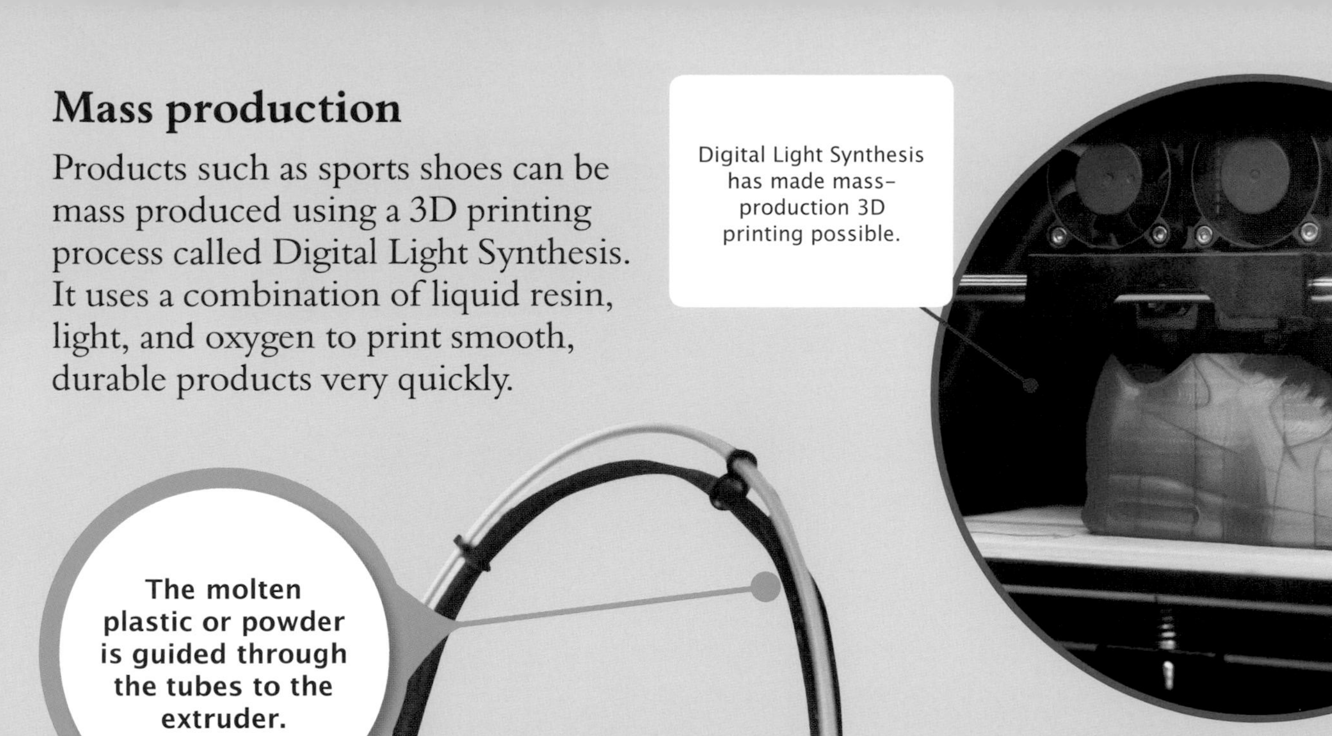
Digital Light Synthesis has made mass-production 3D printing possible.
The molten plastic or powder is guided through the tubes to the extruder.
In the extruder, the material is melted by a heating element, then extruded through a nozzle.
The printing table is usually made of glass.
Motors move the printing table up and down, left to right, and back and forward.

DID YOU KNOW? Food Ink is the world's first touring 3D printing restaurant. The furniture, utensils, and food are created using 3D technology.

Cranes

There are two main types of crane: tower cranes and mobile cranes. Tower cranes are fixed to the ground and are used to build tall buildings. They are built using a mobile crane, which is a crane on the back of a truck. First the mobile crane builds the foundations and adds the tower or mast. The cab and jib are then placed into position. Once a pulley system is in place, the tower crane uses its own hook to build itself taller. It adds one section at a time inside a climbing frame.

A large concrete counterweight balances the load on the jib, stopping the crane from toppling over.

The slewing ring enables the crane to rotate.

Climbing frame
New section

This shows how a tower crane builds itself taller.

Tower

INVENTOR

Inventor: Hans Liebherr

Invention: Mobile crane

Date: 1949

The story: German master builder Hans Liebherr designed and built the first revolving mobile crane. It moved from site to site on the back of a truck, and used hydraulics to lift things.

Pulleys

A tower crane uses several sets of pulleys to lift heavy objects. A steel lifting cable loops around the trolley pulleys and the hook pulley and then over the lifting pulley to a motor. The motor winds the lifting cable in and out of these pulleys to raise and lower the hook.

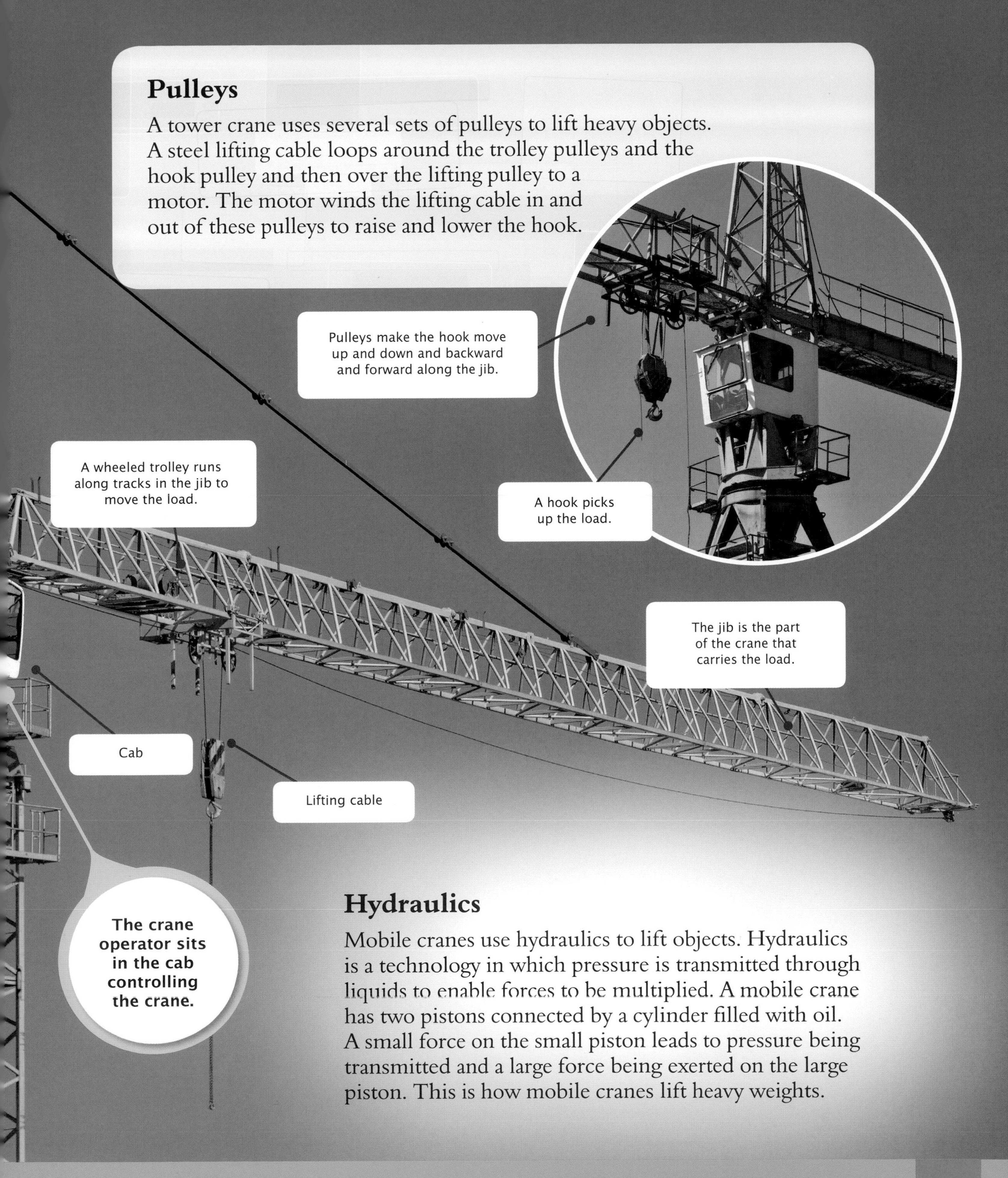

Pulleys make the hook move up and down and backward and forward along the jib.
A wheeled trolley runs along tracks in the jib to move the load.
A hook picks up the load.
The jib is the part of the crane that carries the load.
Cab
Lifting cable
The crane operator sits in the cab controlling the crane.

Hydraulics

Mobile cranes use hydraulics to lift objects. Hydraulics is a technology in which pressure is transmitted through liquids to enable forces to be multiplied. A mobile crane has two pistons connected by a cylinder filled with oil. A small force on the small piston leads to pressure being transmitted and a large force being exerted on the large piston. This is how mobile cranes lift heavy weights.

DID YOU KNOW? The earliest cranes were built by the ancient Greeks.

Traffic Lights

Traffic lights determine right of way at road junctions. Some traffic lights are set with timers, and the lights change after a predetermined length of time. Most, however, are controlled by sensors. These count the number of cars approaching the junction from each direction and keep the busier routes green for longest. Traffic lights are illuminated by SSL lighting (see page 79).

Sensors

With sensor-controlled traffic lights, sensors called induction loops (magnets with loops of wire) are embedded in the road surface. When a car drives over the sensor, it changes the magnetic field and an electrical signal is sent to the computer controlling the traffic light. Each sequence of red-amber-green lights is called a phase. The computer is programmed to let a certain time elapse before a new phase can begin.

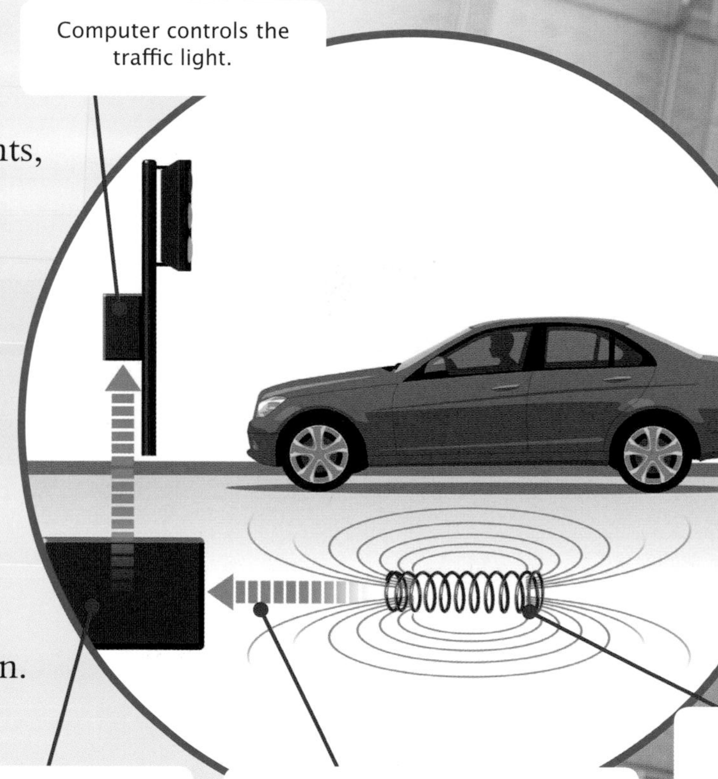
Computer controls the traffic light.
Inductance meter measures the strength of the signal.
When a vehicle is detected, the induction loop sends a signal to the inductance meter.
Two to three induction loops are buried beneath the road surface.

INVENTOR

Inventor: Garrett Morgan

Invention: Traffic lights

Date: 1923

The story: American inventor Garrett Morgan invented the three-position traffic light, adding the amber light. At night, the lights could be set so the amber light blinked to warn drivers to take care at junctions.

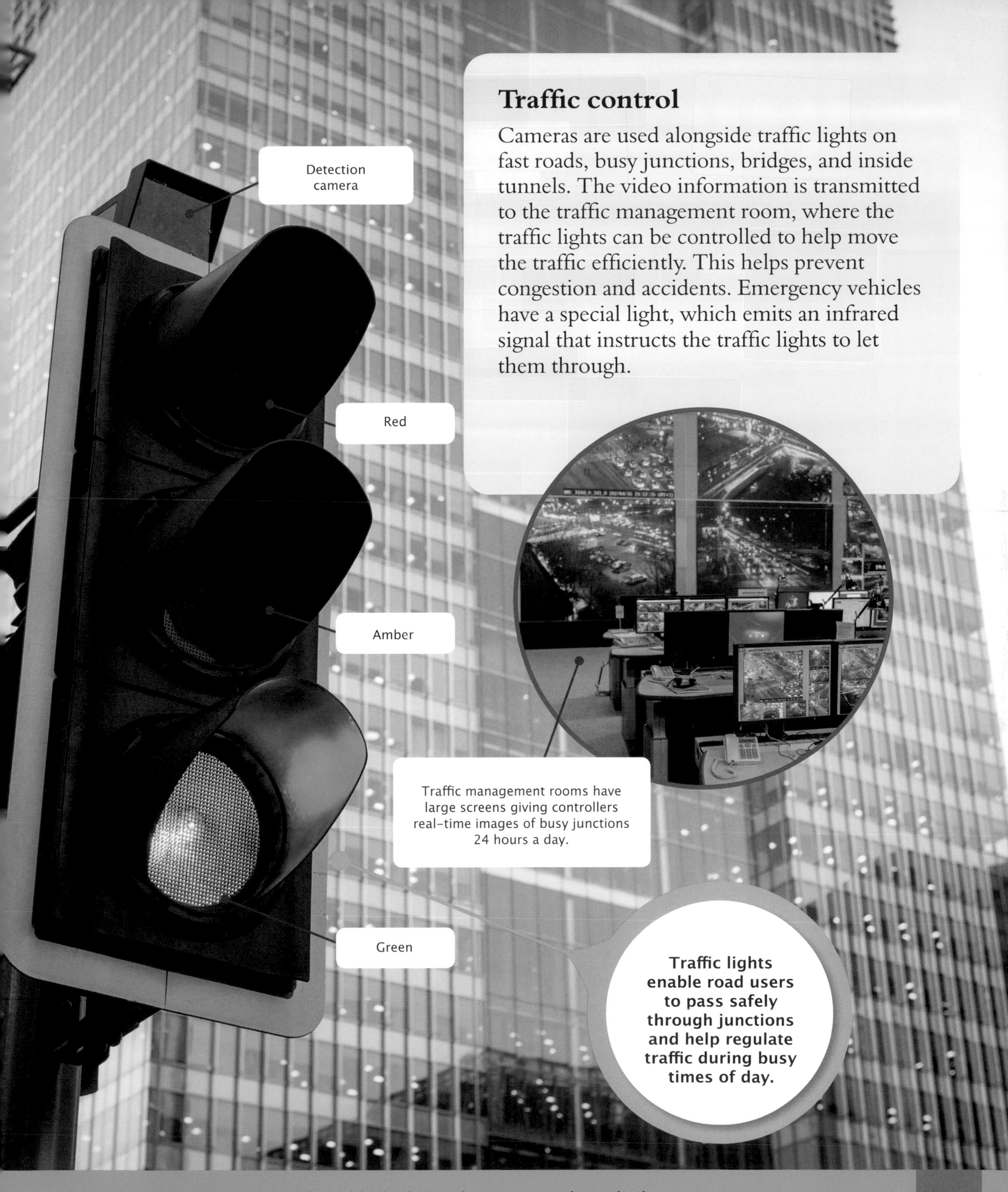
Detection camera
Red
Amber
Green

Traffic control

Cameras are used alongside traffic lights on fast roads, busy junctions, bridges, and inside tunnels. The video information is transmitted to the traffic management room, where the traffic lights can be controlled to help move the traffic efficiently. This helps prevent congestion and accidents. Emergency vehicles have a special light, which emits an infrared signal that instructs the traffic lights to let them through.

Traffic management rooms have large screens giving controllers real-time images of busy junctions 24 hours a day.

Traffic lights enable road users to pass safely through junctions and help regulate traffic during busy times of day.

DID YOU KNOW? Red light has a longer wavelength than green, so it can be seen from further away. This allows for longer braking times.

Printing Presses

Most printing presses work by a process called offset lithography. First, the page to be printed is transferred photographically to a thin metal plate. The image parts of the plate are coated with lacquer so they attract ink, while the rest is coated with gum, so it attracts water. The plate is then curved around a cylinder and covered with water and ink. Only the lacquered parts of the plate pick up ink.

The different inks have to be aligned correctly to produce the perfect print.

Web offset lithography

The inked printing cylinder presses against a soft rubber cylinder called the blanket cylinder, which transfers the image onto paper. Because the printing plate doesn't directly touch the paper, it's called "offsetting." Today's high-speed presses are called "web-fed" because the paper comes into the press from a giant roll called a web.

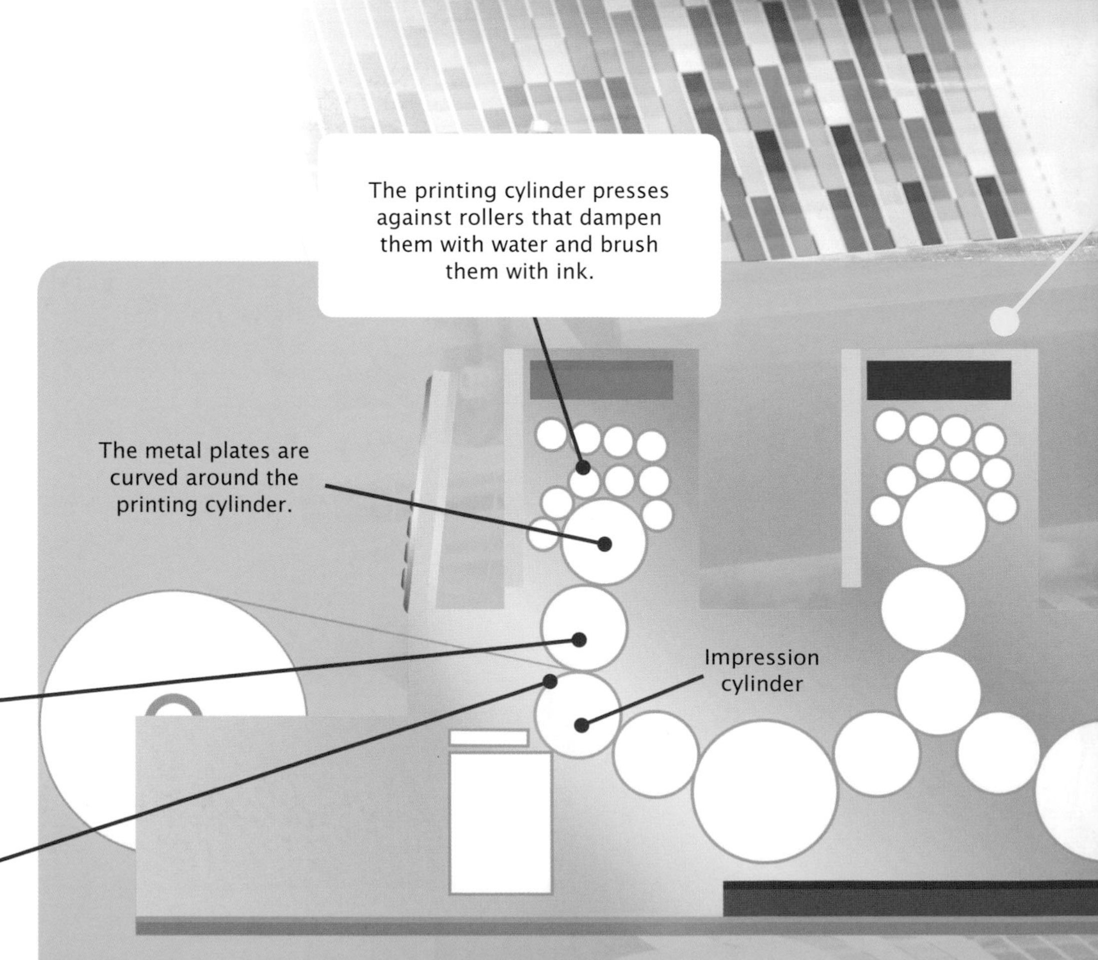
The printing cylinder presses against rollers that dampen them with water and brush them with ink.
The metal plates are curved around the printing cylinder.
Impression cylinder

The blanket cylinder transfers the image to the paper.

Paper feeds between the blanket and impression cylinder.

INVENTOR

Inventor: Johannes Gutenberg

Invention: Printing press

Date: 1450

The story: German blacksmith Johannes Gutenberg invented a form of movable type printing press where individual letters could be moved around to form different texts. A screw-type press stamped the inked metal letters onto the paper.

Computer-to-plate

Modern printing presses use desktop publishing (DTP) software to design where the text and images will go on each page. The digital image is transmitted directly from the computer to a printing plate. The plates are coated with a light-sensitive chemical, then the image areas are burned on with lasers using UV light or heat.

Four shades of ink are printed in sequence—cyan, magenta, yellow, and black. Any shade can be created using these four inks.

Web-fed printing presses can produce around 20 km (12 miles) of printed material in an hour.

Computer-to-plate technology produces higher quality printed material.

DID YOU KNOW? Printing was invented by the Chinese over 1,000 years ago. They carved characters onto wooden blocks, dipped them in ink, and pressed them on parchment to form text.

Wastewater Treatment

Wastewater, or sewage, must be treated so that it does not harm the environment. First comes the "primary treatment." The wastewater flows through a screen to remove large objects, followed by a "grit tank," where sand and small stones settle to the bottom. Then it passes through a sedimentation tank where suspended organic matter settles to the bottom to form sludge. A lot of the sludge is dried and sold to farmers as fertilizer, or else burned to generate electricity.

In some plants, as a secondary treatment, wastewater is passed through a "trickling filter" system.

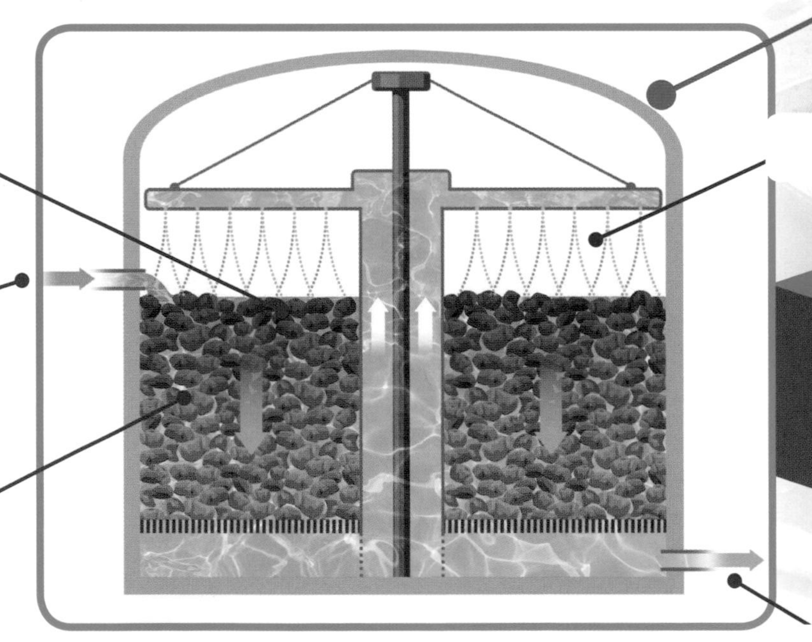

The wastewater is sprayed onto a deep bed of rocks.
Dirty water inlet
The rocks are covered in a slime layer of bacteria that absorb organic matter, purifying the water.
Sprinkler
Clean water outlet

INVENTOR

Inventor: Deepika Kurup

Invention: Solar-powered water purification system

Date: 2012

The story: American Deepika Kurup invented a way to purify water at the age of 14 in her garage. She was inspired by witnessing children in India drinking dirty water. She combined titanium dioxide (TiO_2) with cement. It cleans water by speeding up the sun's disinfection process.

Secondary treatment

After leaving the sedimentation tank, the wastewater is pumped into an aeration tank, where it is mixed with air and "activated" (bacteria-filled) sludge. The bacteria in the sludge breaks down the organic matter remaining in the wastewater and converts it into harmless by-products. The purified liquid waste is then discharged into rivers and streams.

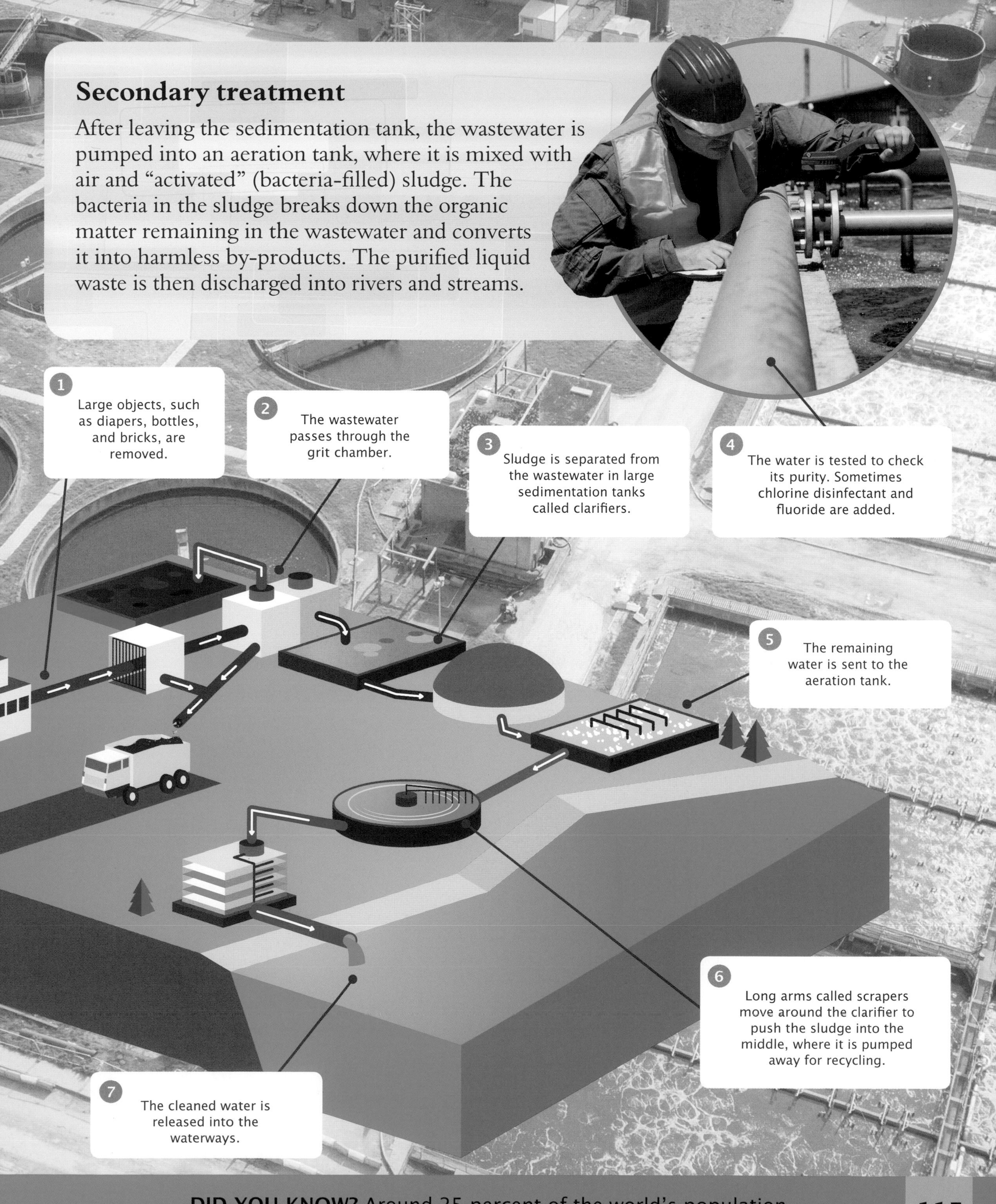

1
Large objects, such as diapers, bottles, and bricks, are removed.
2
The wastewater passes through the grit chamber.
3
Sludge is separated from the wastewater in large sedimentation tanks called clarifiers.
4
The water is tested to check its purity. Sometimes chlorine disinfectant and fluoride are added.
5
The remaining water is sent to the aeration tank.
6
Long arms called scrapers move around the clarifier to push the sludge into the middle, where it is pumped away for recycling.
7
The cleaned water is released into the waterways.

DID YOU KNOW? Around 25 percent of the world's population has no access to clean drinking water.

Nuclear Power

Nuclear power stations produce electricity by splitting uranium atoms in a process called nuclear fission. The heat produced by this process causes water to turn to steam. The high-pressure steam turns a turbine that powers a generator to produce electricity. A by-product of the process is highly radioactive nuclear waste, which must be disposed of safely, usually deep underground.

Safety systems

Nuclear fission takes place in a nuclear reactor. It is a dangerous process. In the reactor's core, fuel rods containing the uranium must be kept immersed in cold water to prevent them from overheating. Control rods are inserted into the core to slow the chain reaction. If the core overheats, coolant is pumped in, or the reactor may be shut down. Otherwise it can lead to an explosion and the release of harmful radiation into the environment.

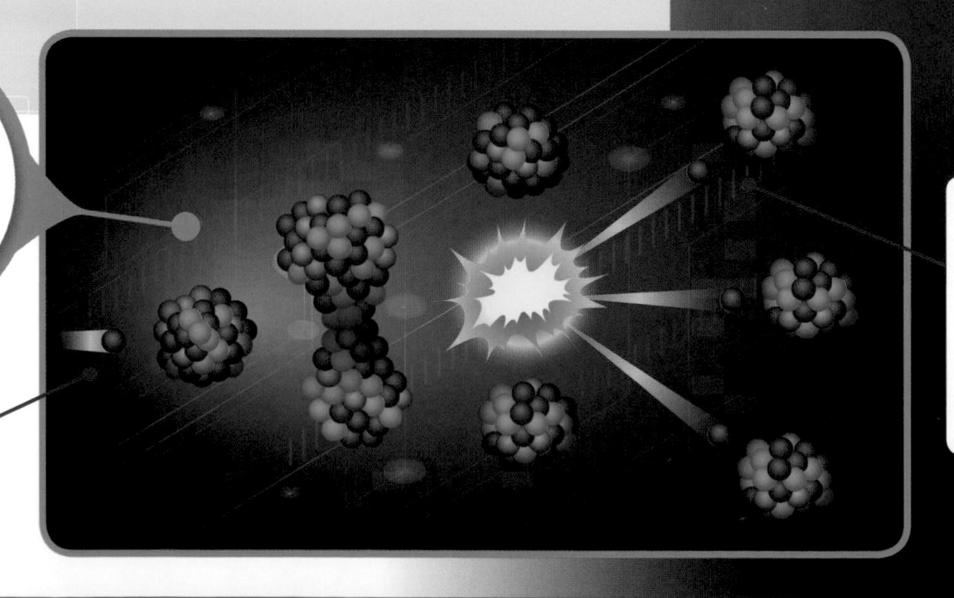

This shows how nuclear fission works.

A neutron from a uranium atom hits the nucleus of another uranium atom, causing it to split.

More neutrons are created, which strike more uranium nuclei, causing a chain reaction.

DID YOU KNOW? The sun is a large nuclear reactor. It uses a natural process of fusion, where four hydrogen nuclei combine to form one helium atom, to produce energy in the form of heat and light.

Coolant, warmed by the reactor, is carried away.

Control rods [green]

Coolant

Large cooling towers release the steam that powers the turbines.

Fuel rods [red]

Radiation protection barrier

Water is stored and pumped around the system to produce steam and maintain temperature.

The containment building contains the reactor and the steam turbine generators.

Pylons carry the high-voltage wires that transfer the electricity over long distances to a substation.

INVENTOR

Inventor: Lise Meitner

Invention: Nuclear fission

Date: 1939

The story: Austrian-Swedish physicist Lise Meitner helped to discover that uranium atoms elongated when bombarded by neutrons, and occasionally some of the uranium atoms would split apart into two smaller, much lighter atoms—barium and krypton—converting mass into energy.

Solar Power

Solar cells convert sunlight into electricity, providing us with a clean, sustainable form of energy. When photons (particles of light) hit a solar cell, they knock electrons free from their atoms. Metal contacts are attached to the positive and negative sides of the cell, forming an electrical circuit. The electrons flow through the circuit, generating electricity.

Solar cells

A solar cell is made from two layers of silicon sandwiched together. The top layer is treated with phosphorus, and the bottom layer with boron. Phosphorus atoms have one too many electrons (they are negatively charged), and boron atoms have one too few (they are positively charged). Photons from sunlight energize the electrons in the top layer, making them jump to the bottom layer. This creates an electrical current.

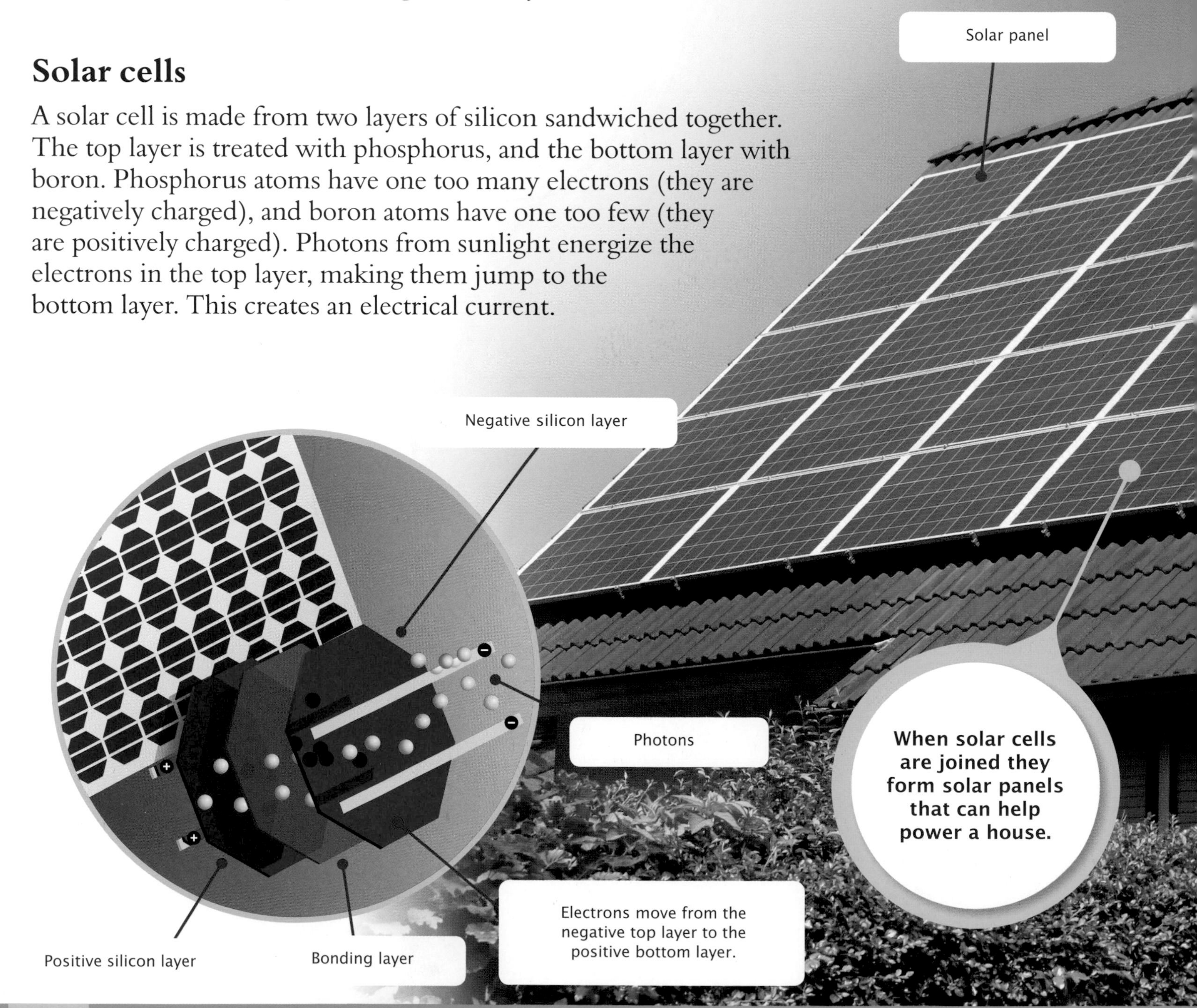

Solar panel
Negative silicon layer
Photons
When solar cells are joined they form solar panels that can help power a house.
Electrons move from the negative top layer to the positive bottom layer.
Positive silicon layer
Bonding layer

DID YOU KNOW? In 2016 Swiss pilot Bertrand Piccard was part of a team that flew a solar-powered plane around the world with no power source other than the sun.

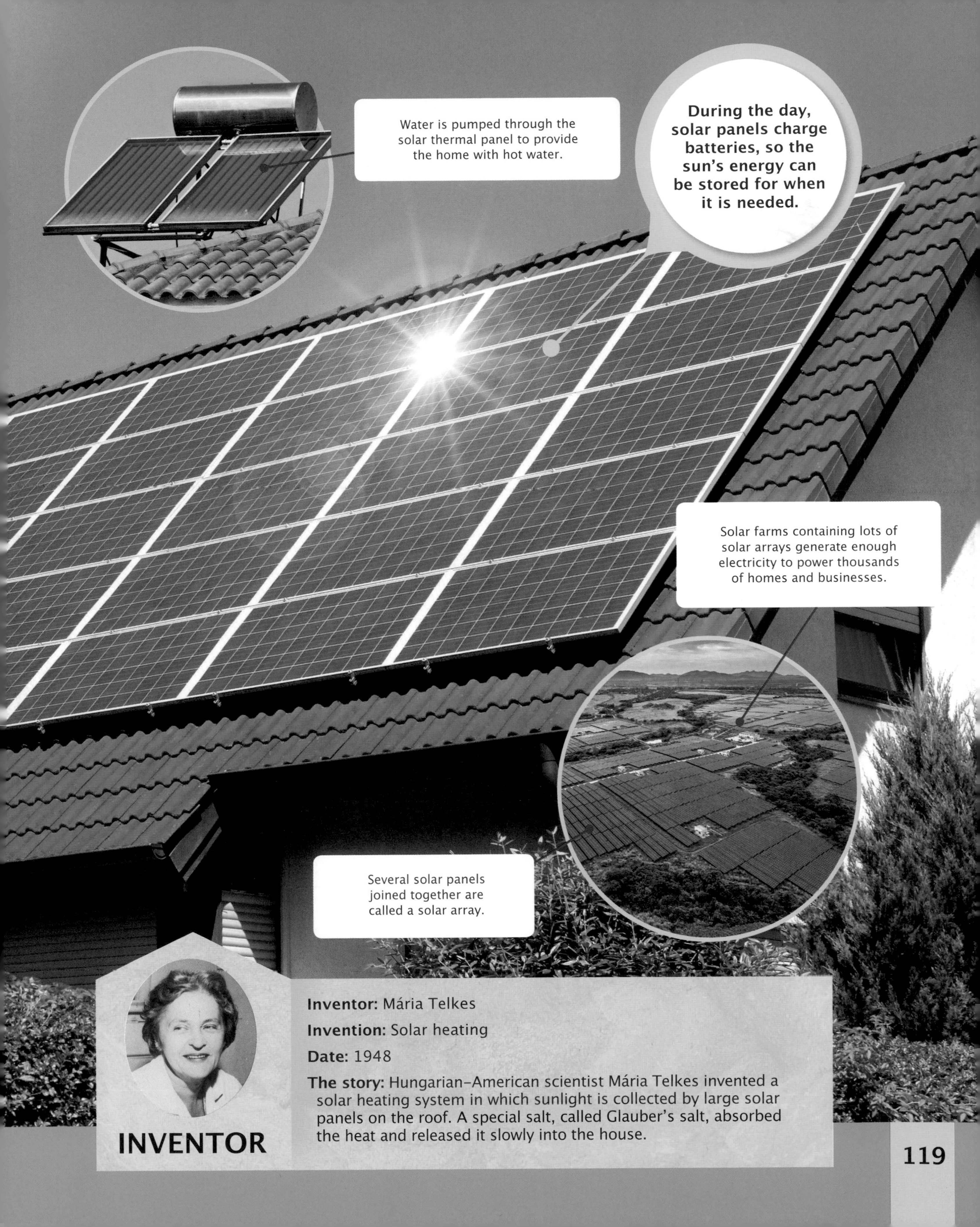
Water is pumped through the solar thermal panel to provide the home with hot water.
During the day, solar panels charge batteries, so the sun's energy can be stored for when it is needed.
Solar farms containing lots of solar arrays generate enough electricity to power thousands of homes and businesses.
Several solar panels joined together are called a solar array.

INVENTOR

Inventor: Mária Telkes

Invention: Solar heating

Date: 1948

The story: Hungarian–American scientist Mária Telkes invented a solar heating system in which sunlight is collected by large solar panels on the roof. A special salt, called Glauber's salt, absorbed the heat and released it slowly into the house.

Recycling Facilities

Materials for recycling are brought to a recycling plant in large trucks. Sometimes the materials have been pre-sorted and sometimes they are sorted at the recycling plant. Trucks empty everything onto conveyor belts. Paper and cardboard are separated by hand into bins to be sent to paper mills. A separator pushes plastic and metal containers onto a side conveyor.

Materials that can be recycled have the international recycling symbol on them.

Magnetic sorters

Metal cans are sorted using magnets. A rotating magnet above the conveyor belt grabs steel metal cans and pulls them into a bin. A magnetized rotor under the conveyor belt repels non-ferrous (non-iron-containing) metal cans, causing them to jump off the belt into another bin.

Plastic
Metal
Glass
Paper

Different materials go into different bins for recycling.

INVENTION

Inventor: Azza Abdel Hamid Faiad

Invention: A catalyst to produce biofuel

Date: 2012

The story: Egyptian Azza Abdel Hamid Faiad discovered a way to recycle plastic waste when she was 16 years old. Her catalyst, aluminosilicate, breaks down plastic waste, producing gases like methane, which can be converted into the biofuel ethanol.

Bales of paper waiting to be recycled
Waste bottles and jars are put into a furnace to be melted down and reused.
Metal is shredded and melted for making into new sheets of metal.
Steel food cans can be melted and made into new cans.
Plastic is the most difficult material to recycle. There are different types of plastics that have to be recycled in different ways.

DID YOU KNOW? It takes less than a week to turn old newspapers, books, and magazines back into new ones.

Robots

Robots are programmable machines that interact with the physical world. Their bodies are made up of movable segments of metal or plastic, connected by joints. Some robots move using actuators. An actuator is part of a machine that is responsible for movement or control. It responds to a control signal that may be an electric current, a pneumatic or hydraulic pressure, or even human power.

A robotic arm is controlled by a computer program to repeatedly perform a precise set of movements.

Forearm rotates

Whole arm rotates

Elbow bends

Shoulder swivels

Solar panel provides power
Antenna for communication
Camera
Wheels for rough terrain

Mars Exploration Rovers are mobile robots programmed to explore and analyze the surface of Mars.

Sensory systems

Simple mobile robots use infrared or ultrasound sensors to “see” and avoid obstacles. Sound or light beams are reflected off objects to identify their distance. More advanced robots use stereo vision—two cameras give them a 3D view of the world around them. Image-recognition software enables them to locate and identify objects. Some also use microphones and smell sensors.

INVENTION

Inventor: George Devol

Invention: Robotic arm

Date: 1961

The story: American inventor George Devol designed a mechanical arm that could be programmed to repeat precise tasks like grasping and lifting. His invention revolutionized production lines around the world.

Grippers contain pressure sensors, so they don't crush car parts.
Other arms operate tools such as welding torches and paint sprayers.
Robotic arm holds the car panel precisely in place.
Arms can handle small parts and tighten screws.

Swarm robots

Today, scientists are creating and testing tiny swarm robots. They work together and communicate (using infrared light) in order to carry out tasks, similar to bee and ant colonies. Some can also fit together to make one larger machine.

DID YOU KNOW? The first industrial robot was built in 1961 and was called Unimate. It stacked sheets of burning hot metal used in car production. It opened the door for robot assembly lines.

Artificial Intelligence

Artificial intelligence is the use of computer algorithms (sets of rules) to perform tasks that usually require human intelligence, such as problem-solving, understanding language, and logical reasoning. First, a computer gathers data through sensors or human input. Then the AI program compares this to stored data, works out what it signifies, and decides on a course of action. The value of AI is that computers can usually perform these tasks much more quickly than humans.

Computer chess engines can analyze hundreds of millions of moves per second, enabling them to beat any human grandmaster.

She has cameras in her eyes, combined with algorithms, enabling her to maintain eye contact and recognize people.

Machine Learning

Sometimes computers are used to identify patterns and anomalies in a mass of data. This can help them identify spam email, financial fraud, objects in a scene, or certain words in a speech. It requires them to make decisions based on probability. This form of AI is called machine learning, because it can learn and improve from experience without being programmed to do so. There is, however, a danger that they can repeat the biases (prejudices) of their human programmers.

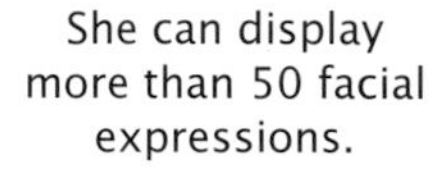
She can display more than 50 facial expressions.

Sophia the robot is programmed to learn.

She can process speech and have conversations using natural language.

Humanoid robots

Some robots are built to look and act like humans. Pepper is the first humanoid robot capable of recognizing human emotions and adapting his responses accordingly. Pepper was created to communicate in natural and intuitive ways, through body movements and voice.

pepper

Pepper expresses itself through arm movements, changing the colour of its eyes, its tablet, and the tone of its voice.

INVENTOR

Inventor: Herbert A. Simon (pictured) and Allen Newell

Invention: General Problem Solver

Date: 1958

The story: Herbert A. Simon and Allen Newell created the General Problem Solver, which solved problems through trial and error by analyzing end results. It was a major step toward artificial intelligence.

DID YOU KNOW? On October 25, 2017, Sophia the robot was granted Saudi Arabian citizenship.

Glossary

AERATION
The process by which air is circulated through, mixed with, or dissolved in a liquid or substance.

AILERON
A hinged surface in the trailing edge of an aircraft wing, used to control the roll of an aircraft.

AMPLIFIER
A device for increasing the amplitude (size) of electrical signals, especially in sound reproduction.

ANALOG
Describes a device that represents signals or data as continuously variable quantities (often contrasted with DIGITAL).

ANTENNA
A rod, dish, or other structure by which radio signals are transmitted or received.

BINARY CODE
A coding system in which binary numbers (zeroes and ones) are used to program a digital computer.

BIOFUEL
A fuel obtained from living or recently living biological material.

CAPACITOR
A device used to store an electric charge, consisting of one or more pairs of conductors separated by an insulator.

CENTRAL PROCESSING UNIT
The part of a computer in which operations are controlled and executed.

CIRCUIT
A path an electrical current can flow along.

CONCAVE
Having a surface that curves inward, like the interior of a sphere.

CONDUCTOR
A material that enables the flow of heat or electricity.

CONVEX
Having a surface that curves outward, like the exterior of a sphere.

DIAPHRAGM
A taut, flexible sheet of material used in certain devices.

DIGITAL
Describes a device that expresses signals or data as series of the digits 0 and 1 (often contrasted with ANALOG).

DNA
Deoxyribonucleic acid (DNA) is a self-replicating material present in nearly all living organisms. It is the carrier of genetic information.

ELECTRODE
A conductor through which electricity enters or leaves an object.

ELECTROMAGNETIC RADIATION
Radiation on any of a range of wavelengths, including visible light, radio waves, microwaves, and X-rays.

ELECTRON
A particle within an atom that carries a negative electrical charge.

EXHAUST
Waste gases expelled from an engine or other machine.

EXTRUDE
Thrust or force out through a nozzle.

FILAMENT
A piece of thin, coiled wire.

FREQUENCY
The number of times a wave completes a cycle in a second. Frequency is measured in hertz (Hz).

FRICTION
The resistance that one surface or object encounters when moving over another.

HARD DRIVE
A device that permanently stores and retrieves data on a computer.

INDUCTION
The production of an electric current through nearness (without contact) of an electrified or magnetized body.

INFRARED
Having a wavelength greater than that of the red end of the visible light spectrum but less than that of microwaves.

INTEGRATED CIRCUIT
An electronic circuit formed on a piece of semiconducting material.

LASER
A device that generates an intense beam of light through the emission of photons from excited atoms or molecules.

LUBRICATION
The application of a substance such as oil to an engine or device to minimize friction and aid smooth movement.

MAGNETIC FIELD
A region around a magnet within which the force of magnetism acts.

MICROWAVES
Having a wavelength shorter than that of a radio wave, but longer than that of infrared radiation.

OPERATING SYSTEM
The software that supports a computer's basic functions.

PHOTON
A particle representing a discrete quantity of light.

PISTON
A disc that fits within a cylinder and moves up and down against a liquid or gas. It forms part of an internal-combustion engine or pump.

PROSTHETIC
Describing an artificial body part.

PROTON
A particle within an atom that carries a positive electrical charge.

PULLEY
A wheel with a grooved rim around which a cord passes. It is used to change the direction of a force applied to the cord, to raise heavy weights.

RADIATION
The emission of energy in the form of electromagnetic waves.

RADIOACTIVE
Emitting radiation in the form of ionized particles (particles stripped of one or more electrons).

REFRIGERANT
A substance used in refrigeration that changes from liquid to gas and back again. Common refrigerants include ammonia and propane.

ROUTER
A device that forwards data packets (formatted units of data) to different parts of a computer network.

RUDDER
A flat piece hinged vertically near the stern of a boat for steering.

SEMICONDUCTOR
A substance, like silicon, that displays variable resistance to an electrical current, useful for electronic circuits.

SENSOR
A device that detects, measures, or records an external activity or event.

SERVER
A computer program or device that provides services to other devices, such as data storage or sharing.

SOFTWARE
The programs and operating systems used by a computer.

SPOILER
A flap on the wing of an aircraft that can be deployed to create drag and reduce speed.

TELECOMMUNICATION
Communication over a distance by, for example, wire or radio signals.

TERMINAL
A point of connection for closing an electric circuit.

THERMOSTAT
A device that automatically regulates temperature or activates a device when the temperature reaches a certain point.

TOMOGRAPHY
A technique for displaying a cross-section through a human body or some other solid object using X-rays or ultrasound.

TRANSISTOR
A tiny device that can amplify or switch an electronic signal.

TURBINE
A rotor that is turned by the flow of wind, water, steam, or some other fluid in order to generate power.

ULTRASOUND
Sound waves with a frequency above the upper limit of human hearing.

ULTRAVIOLET
Having a wavelength shorter than that of the violet end of visible light, but longer than that of X-rays.

USB
Universal serial bus (USB) is a standard technology for connecting devices to a computer.

VACUUM
A space from which the air has been removed.

VALVE
A device for controlling the passage of fluid through a pipe or duct.

VOLTAGE
A measure of the force of an electrical charge as it moves in a wire or other electrical conductor.

WAVELENGTH
The distance between successive crests of an electromagnetic wave.

Index